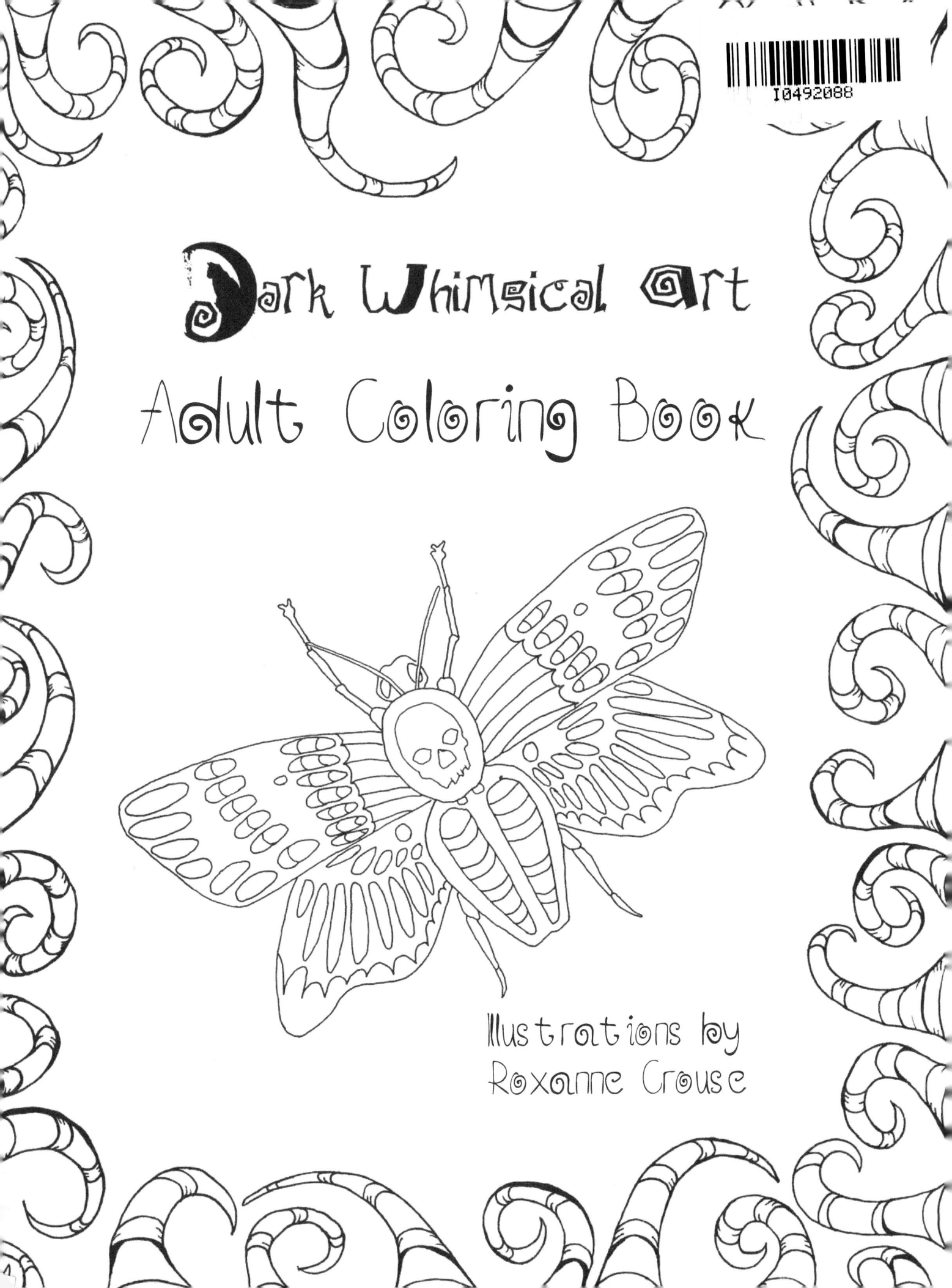

Dark Whimsical Art

Adult Coloring Book

Illustrations by
Roxanne Crouse

Use This Page To Test Your Colors

Dark Whimsical Art Coloring Book

Copyright 2018 Roxanne Crouse

Published by Dark Whimsical Art
Email: photogoorooatyahoo.com
Website: www.darkwhimsicalart.com

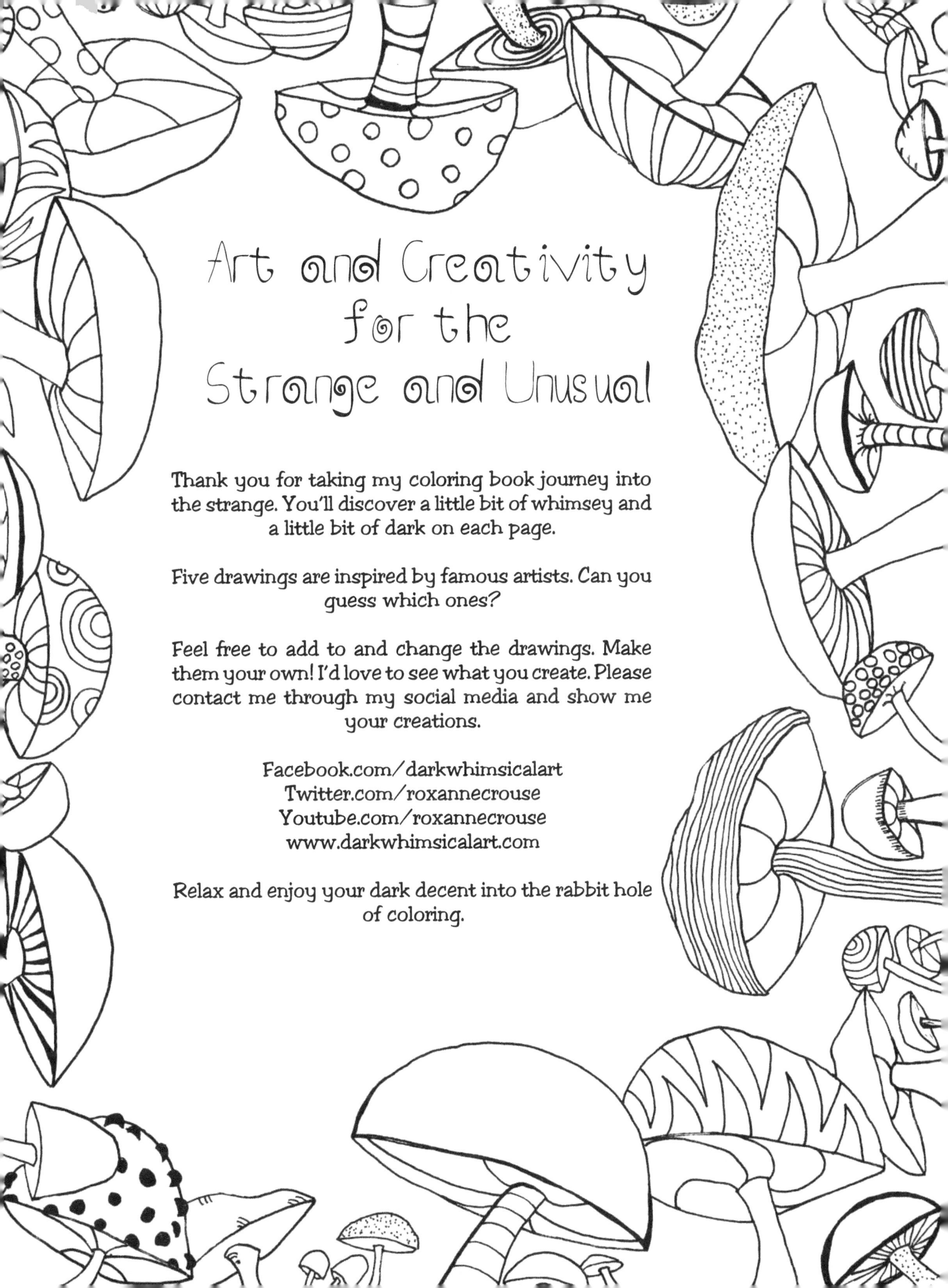

Art and Creativity for the Strange and Unusual

Thank you for taking my coloring book journey into the strange. You'll discover a little bit of whimsey and a little bit of dark on each page.

Five drawings are inspired by famous artists. Can you guess which ones?

Feel free to add to and change the drawings. Make them your own! I'd love to see what you create. Please contact me through my social media and show me your creations.

Facebook.com/darkwhimsicalart
Twitter.com/roxannecrouse
Youtube.com/roxannecrouse
www.darkwhimsicalart.com

Relax and enjoy your dark decent into the rabbit hole of coloring.

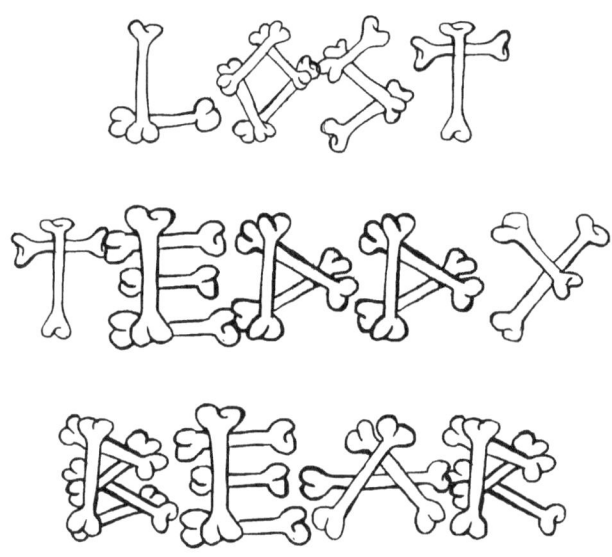

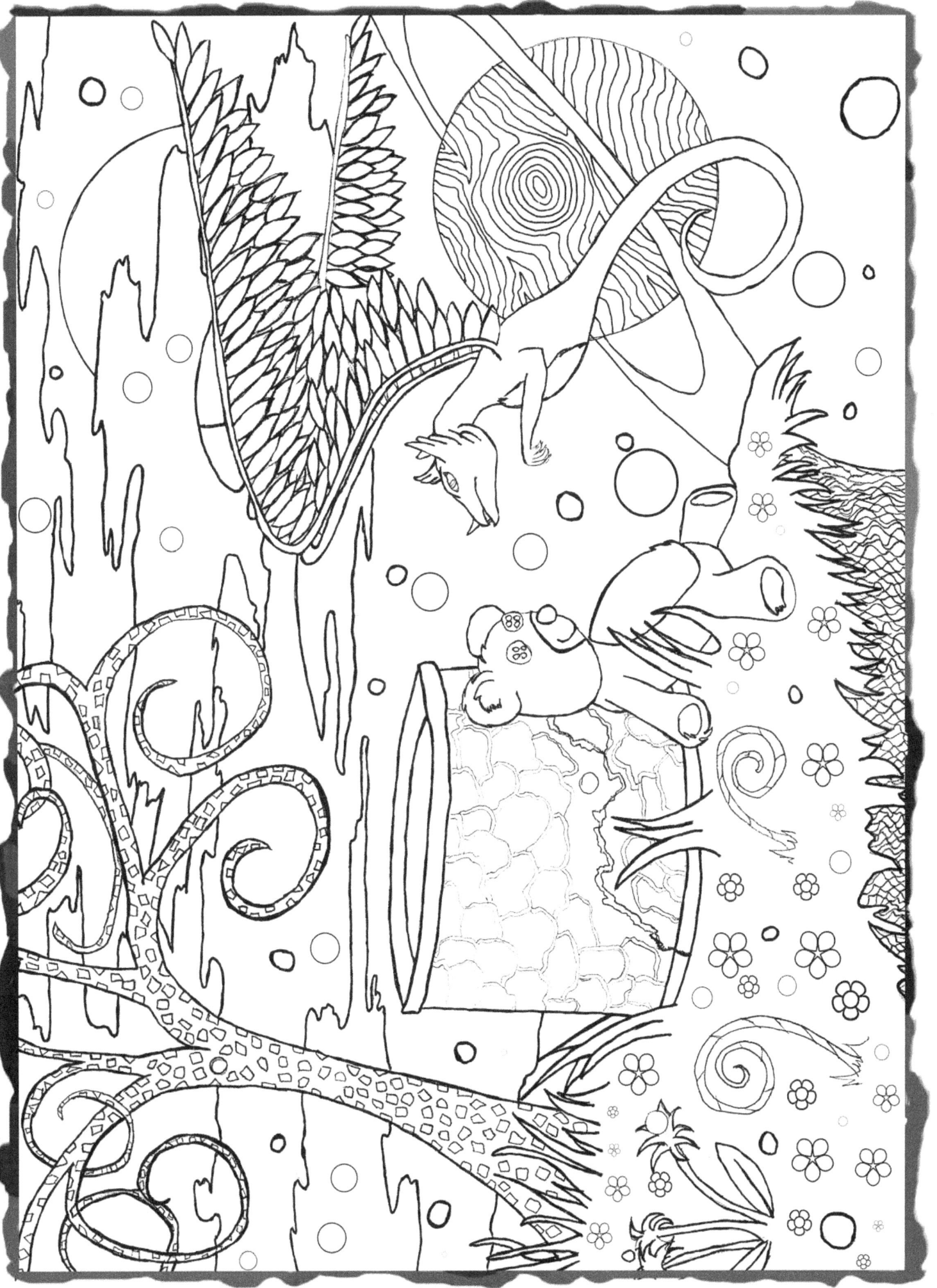

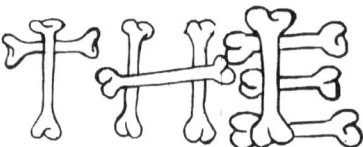

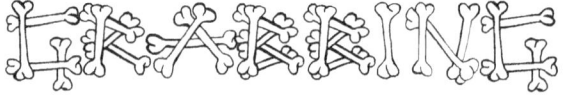

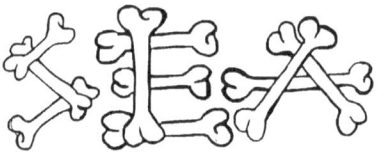

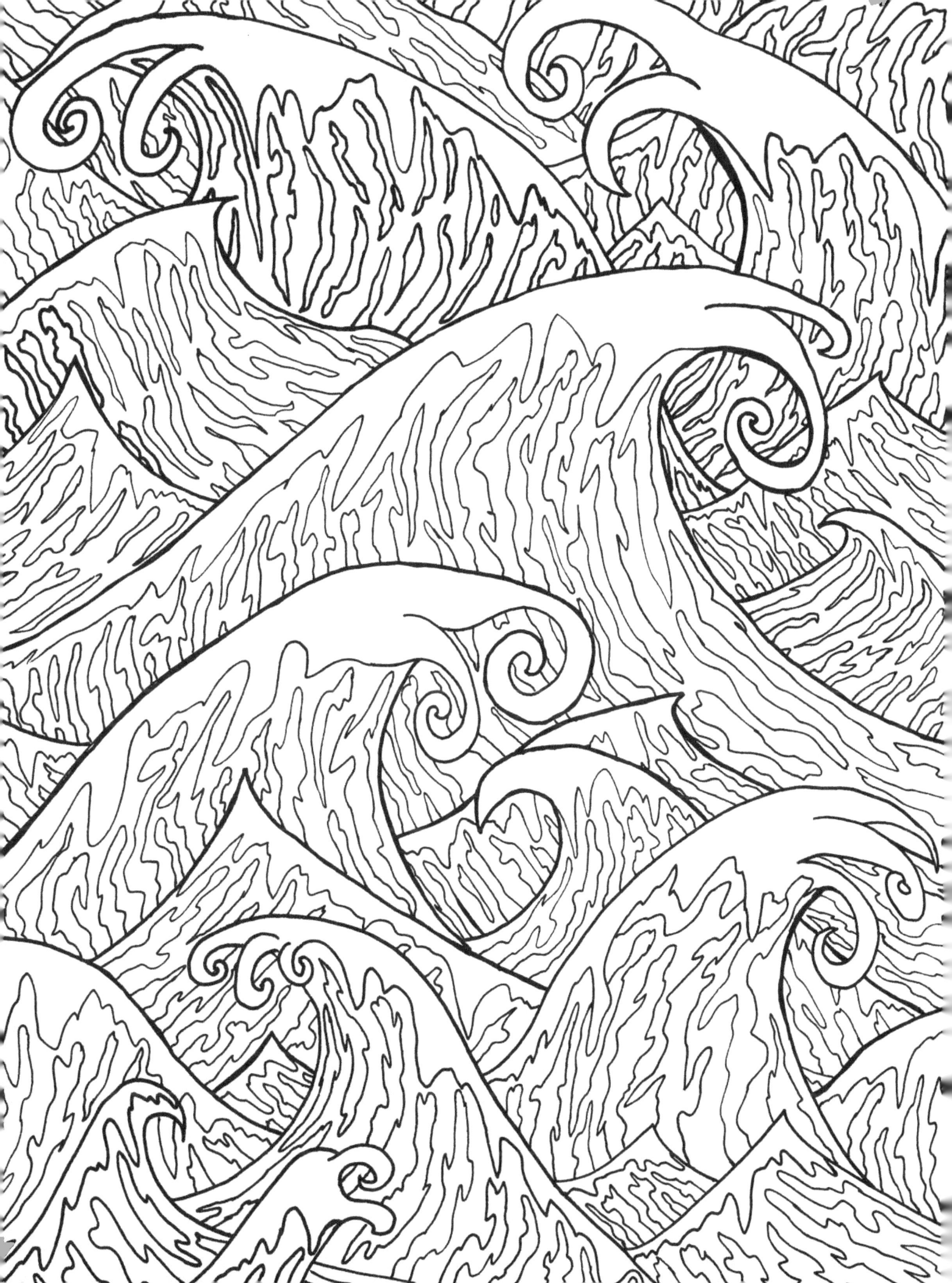

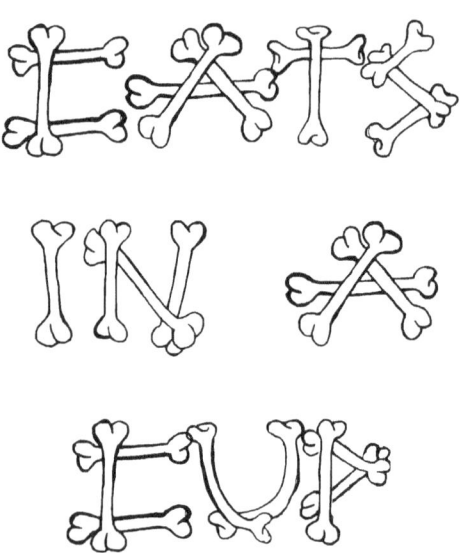

EATS
IN A
CUP

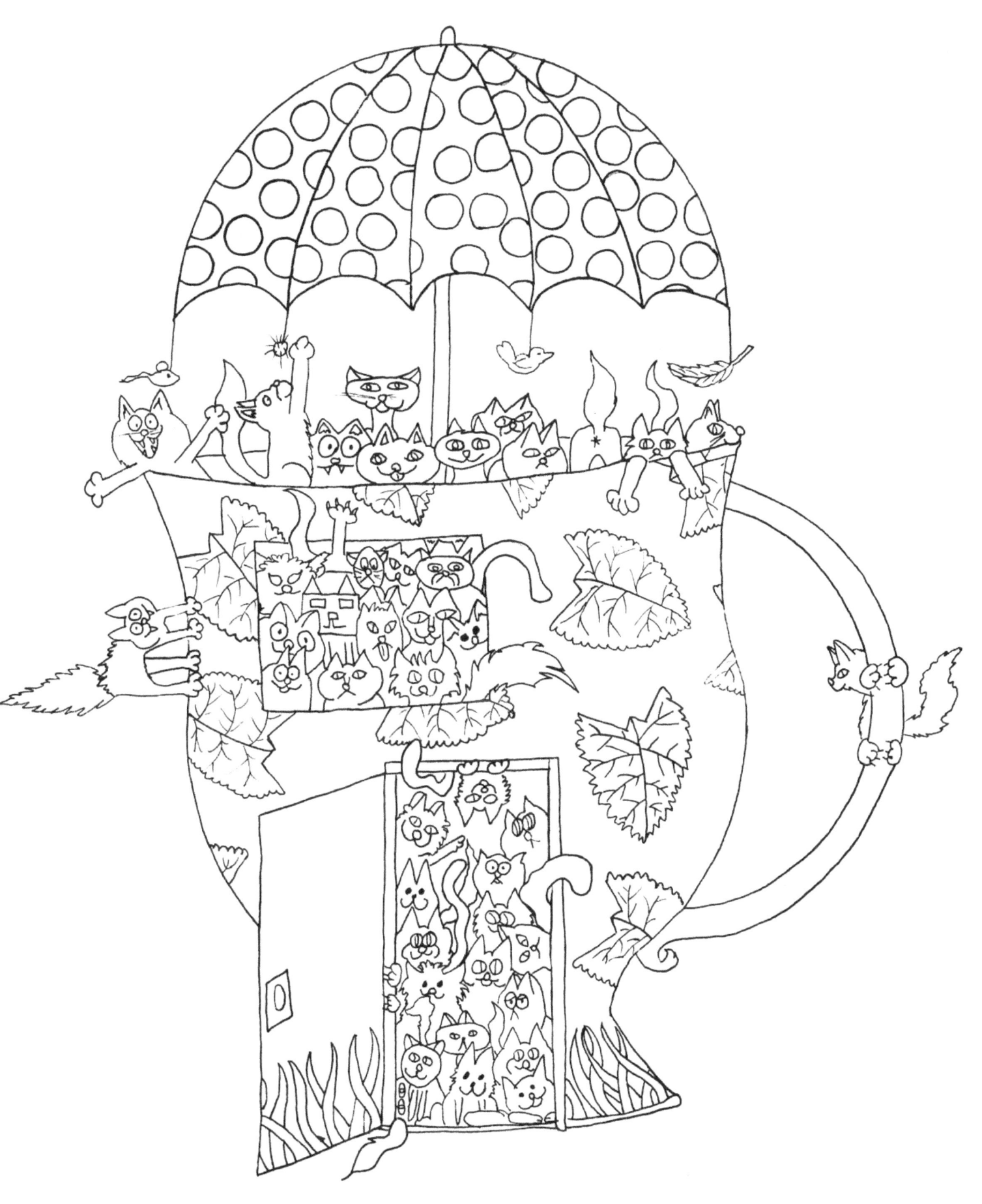

THE

PERSISTENCE

OF

MEOWING

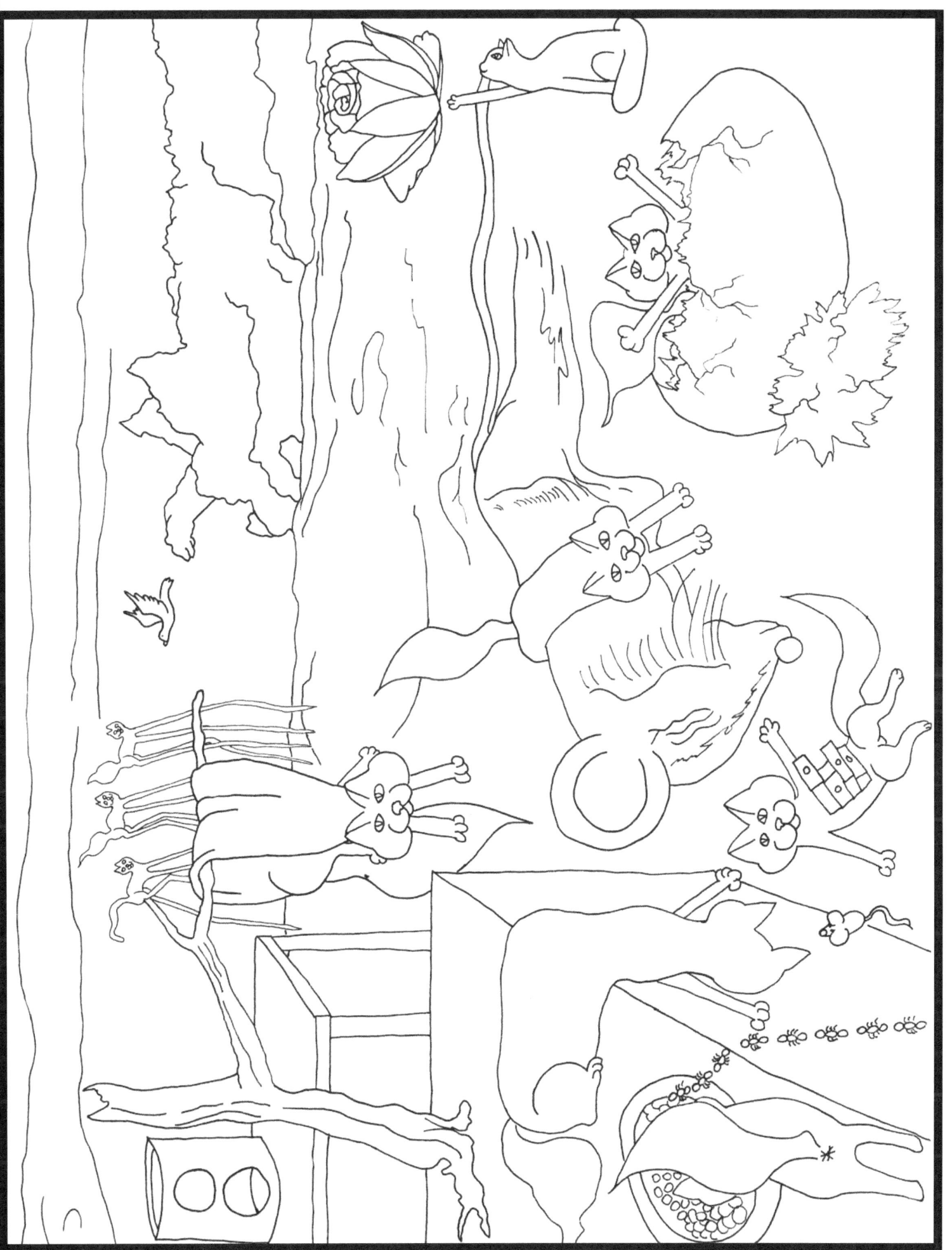

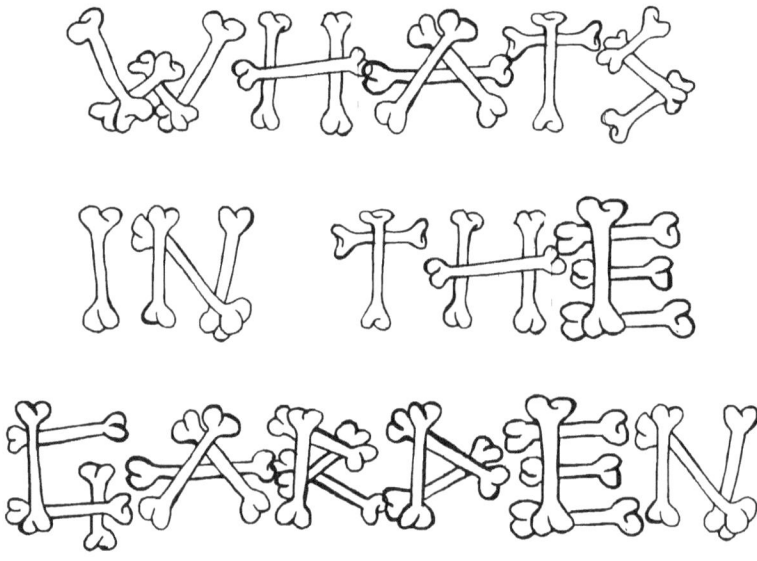

WHATS
IN THE
GARDEN

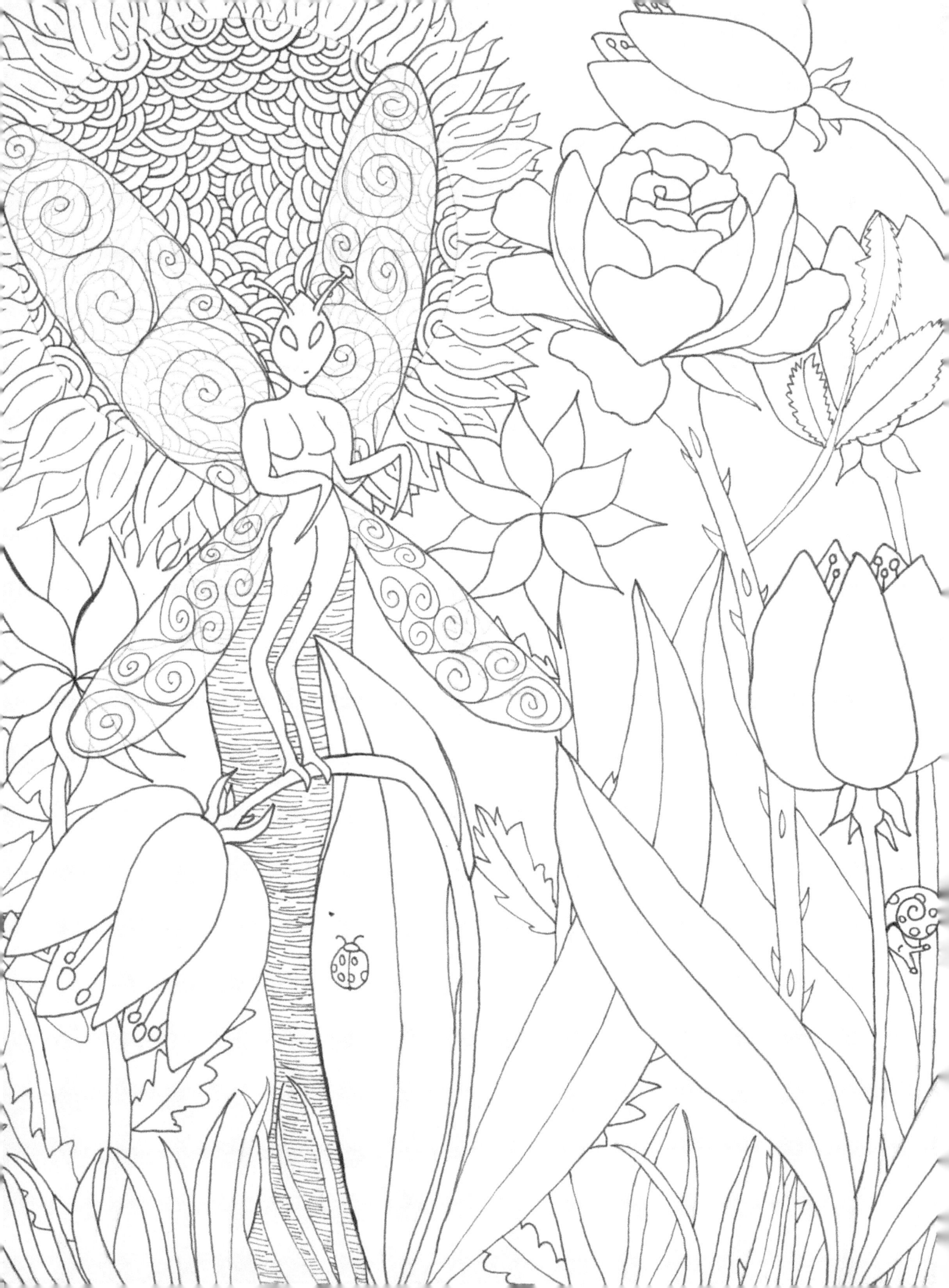

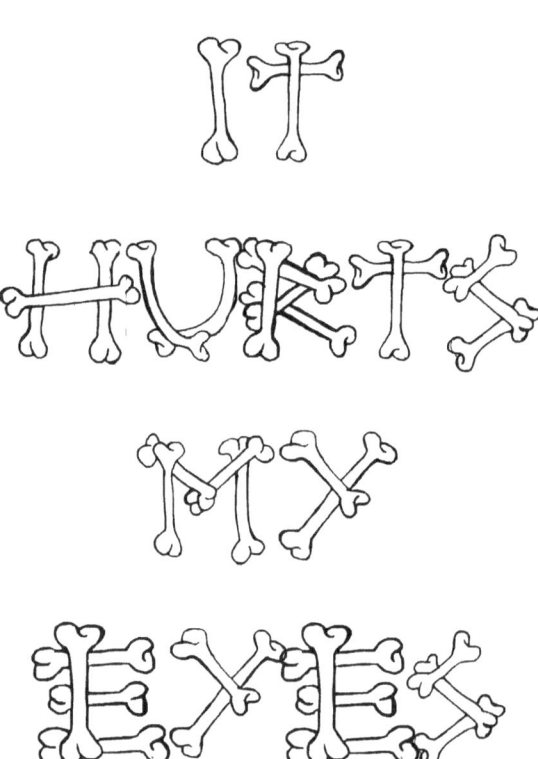

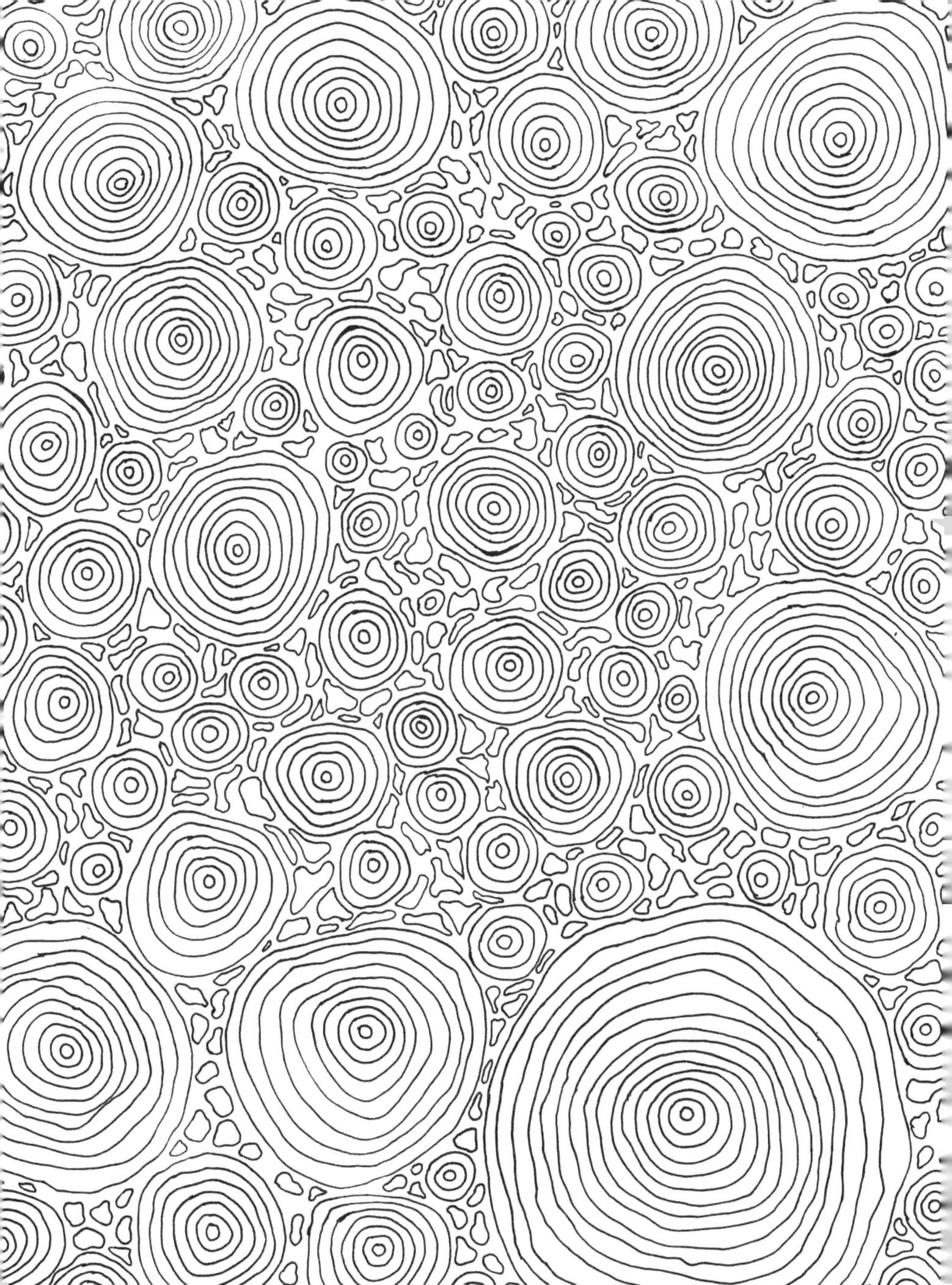

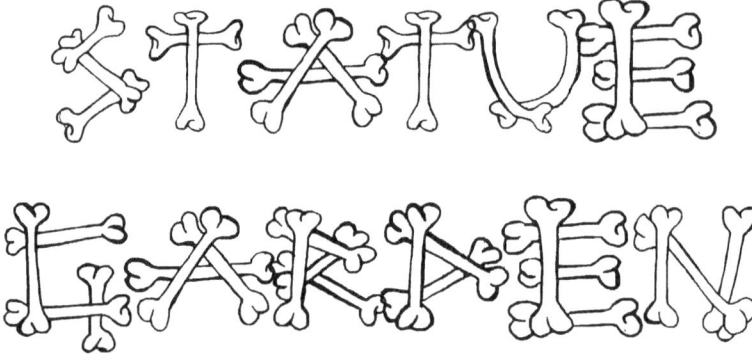

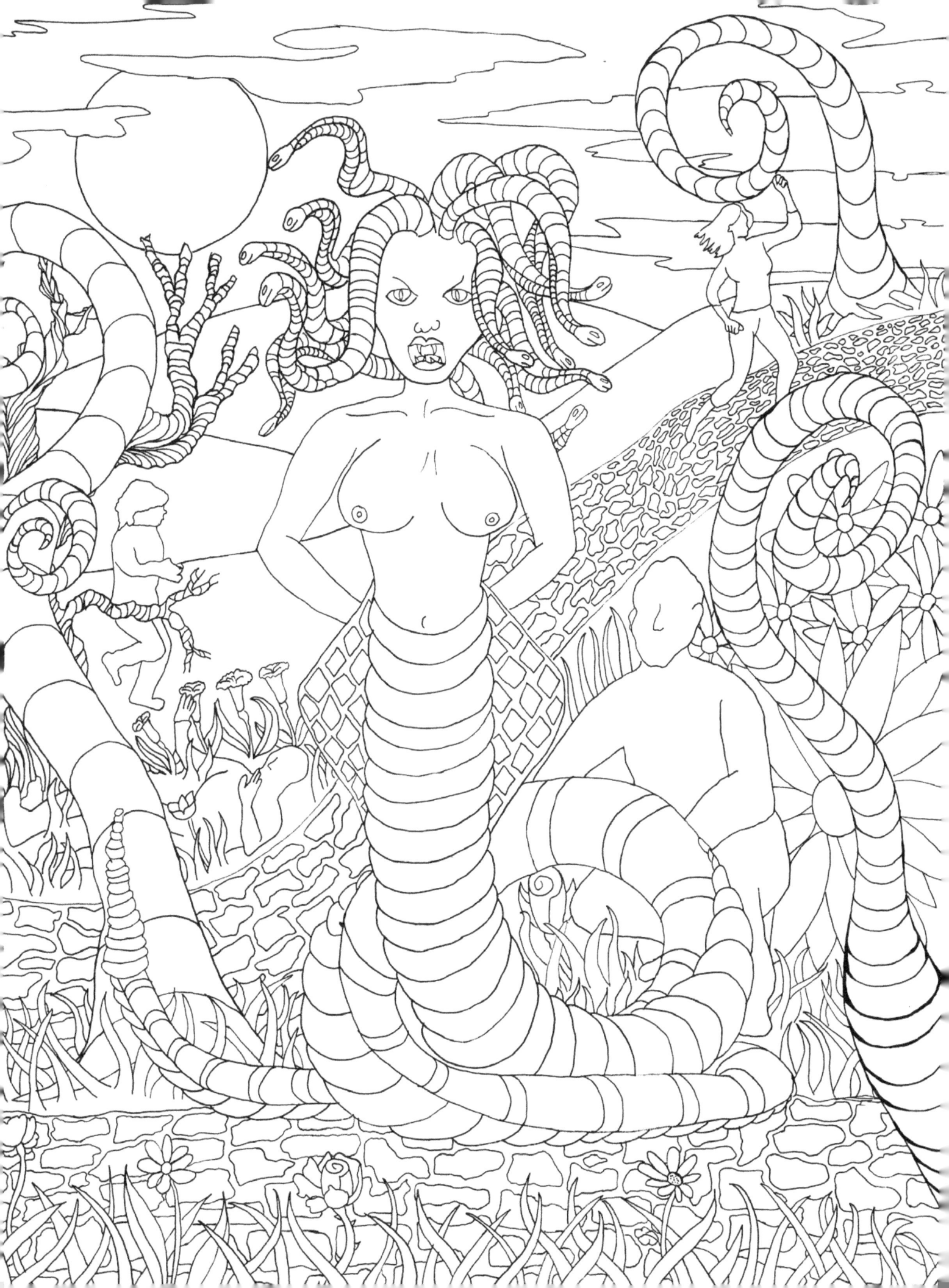

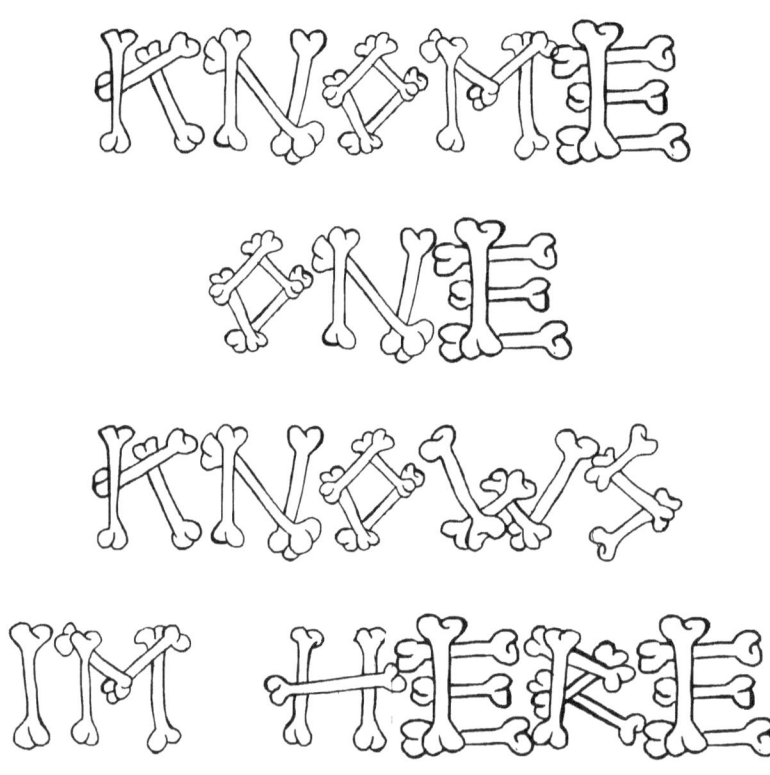

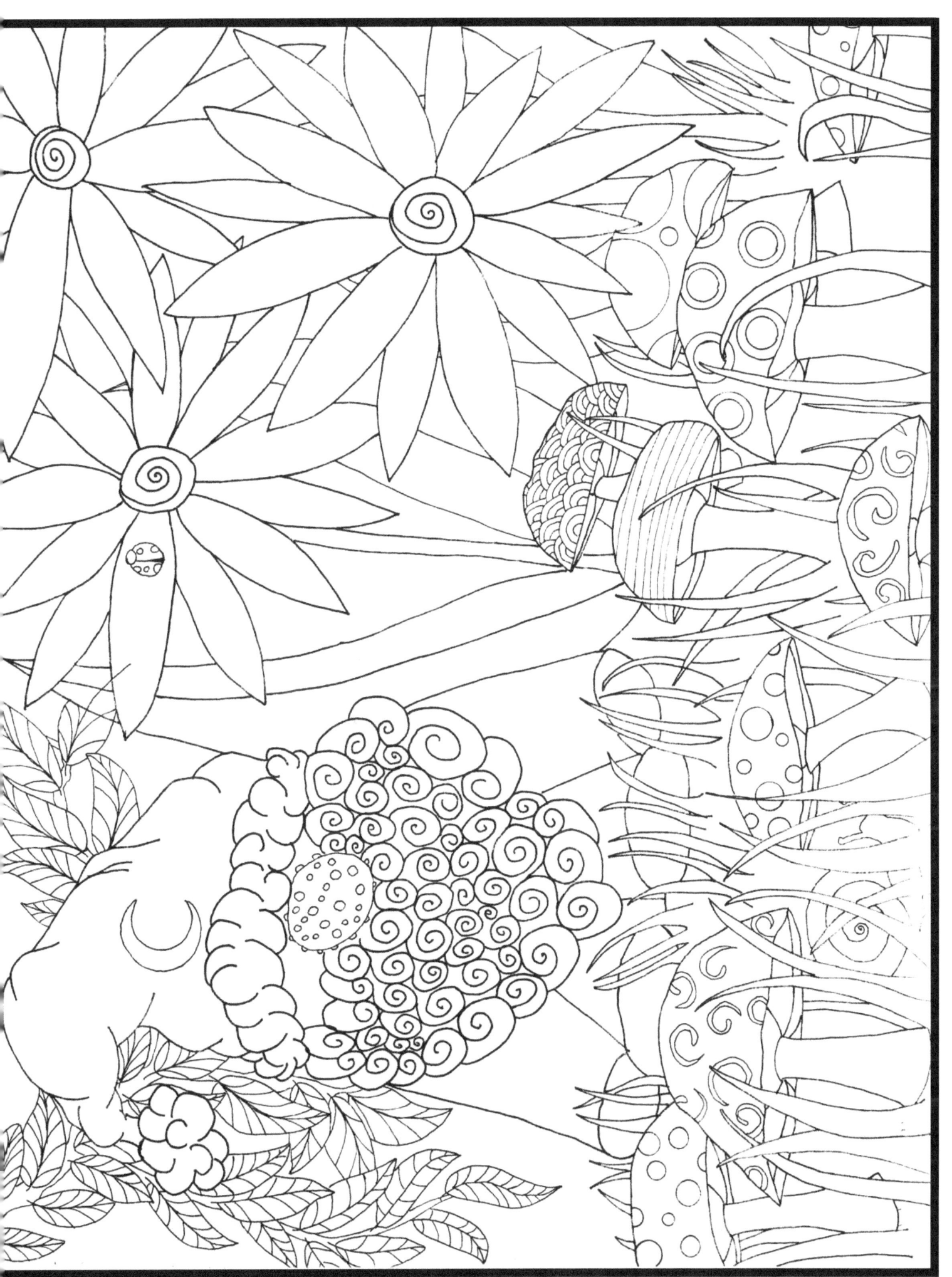

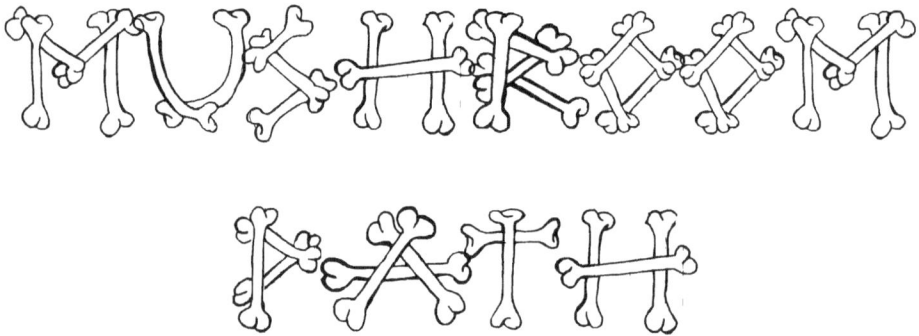

MUSHROOM PATH

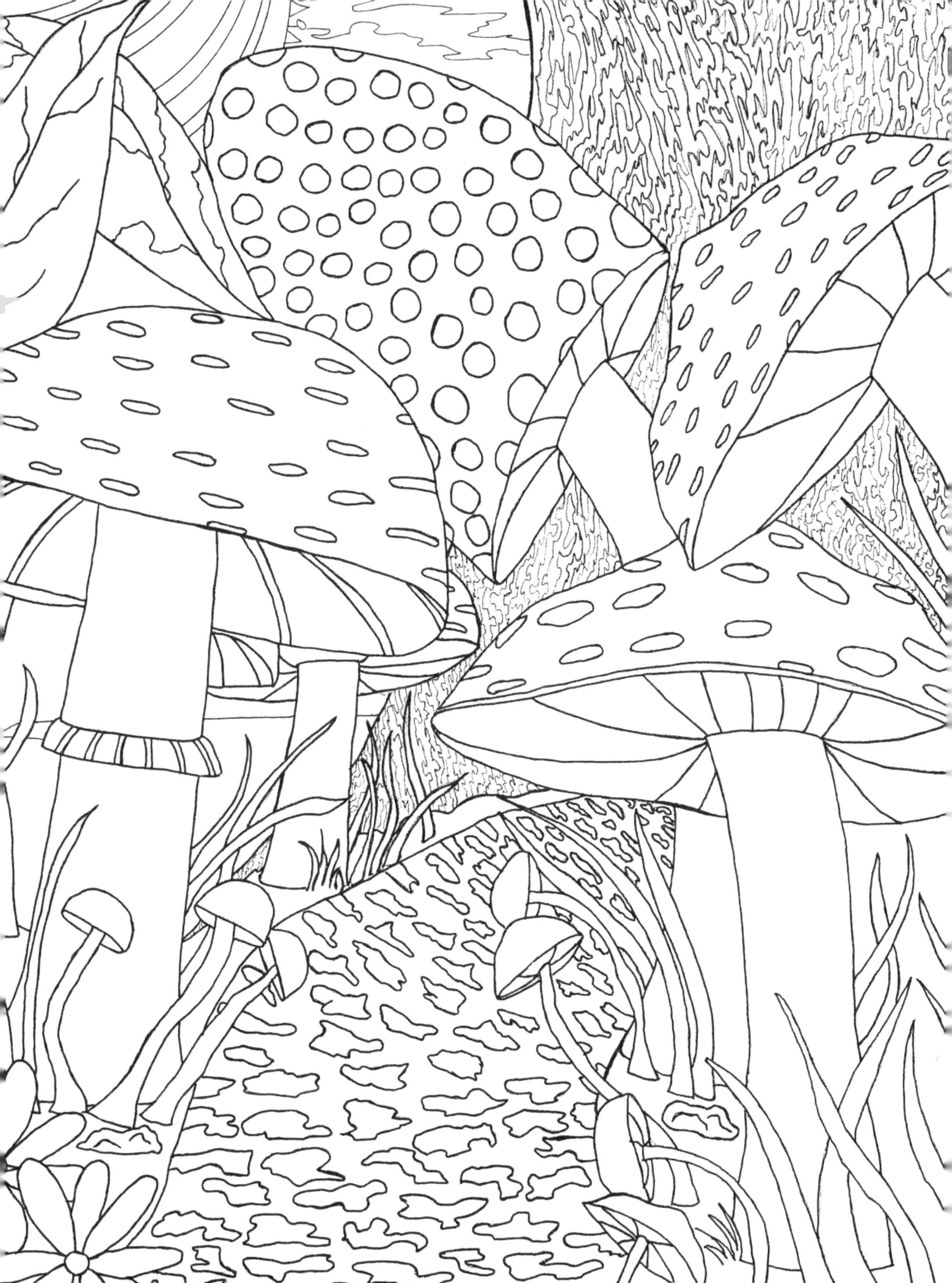

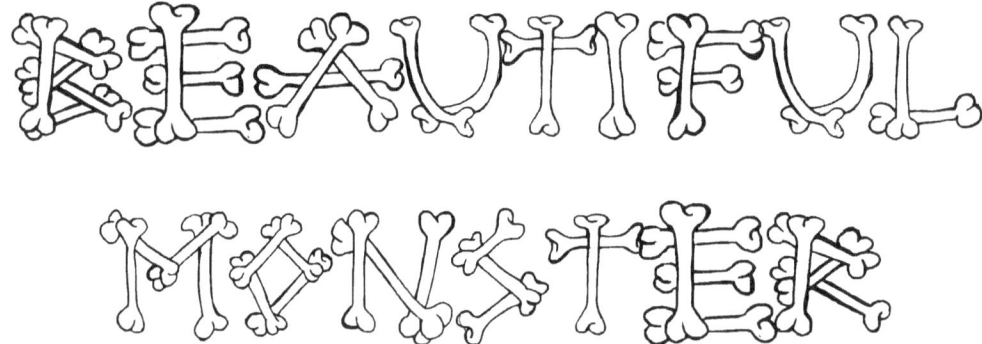

BEAUTIFUL MONSTER

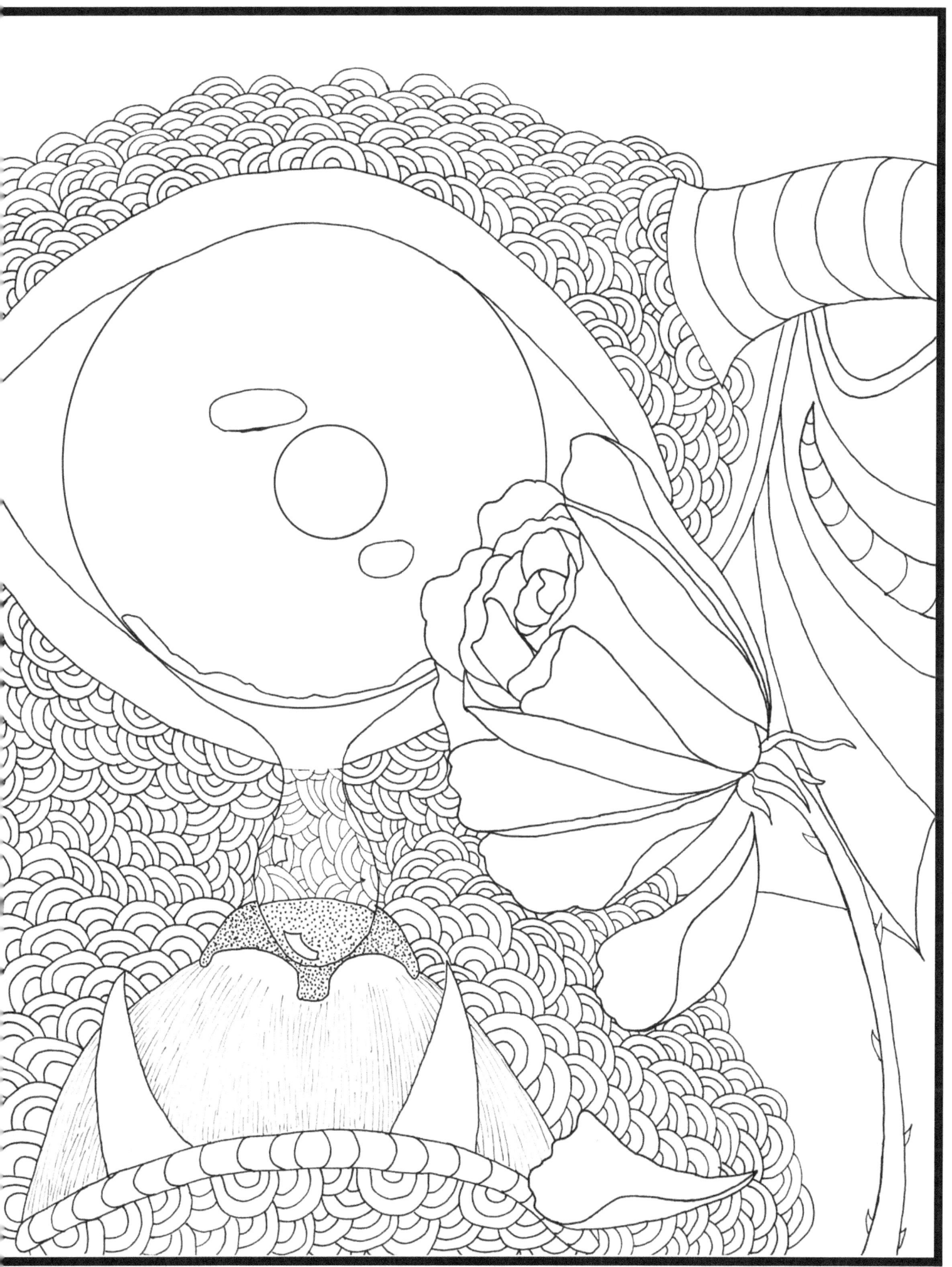

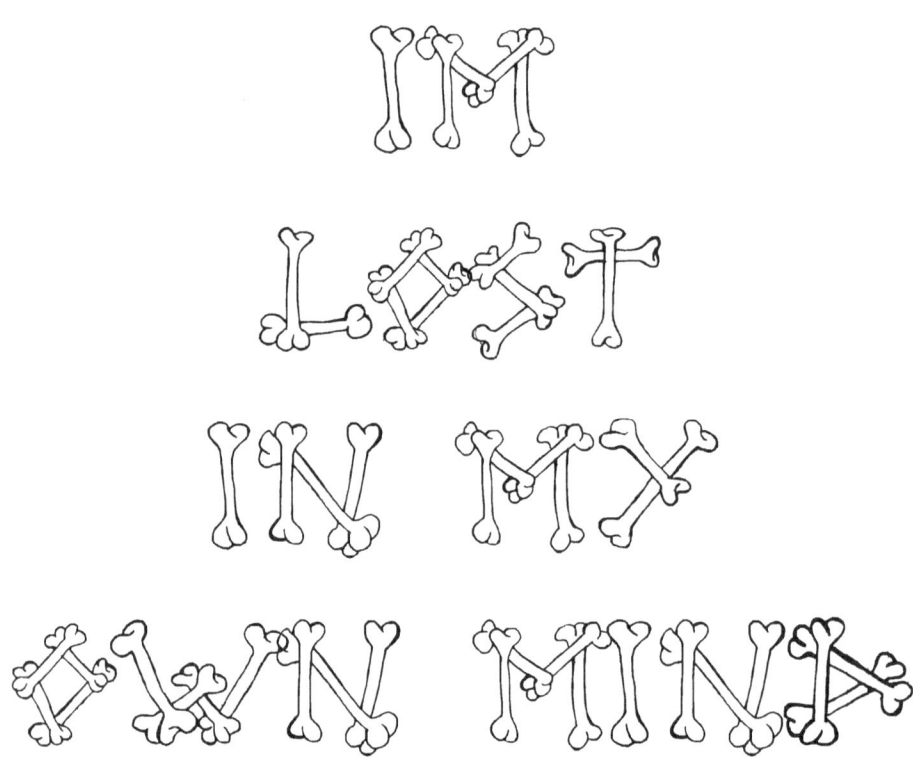

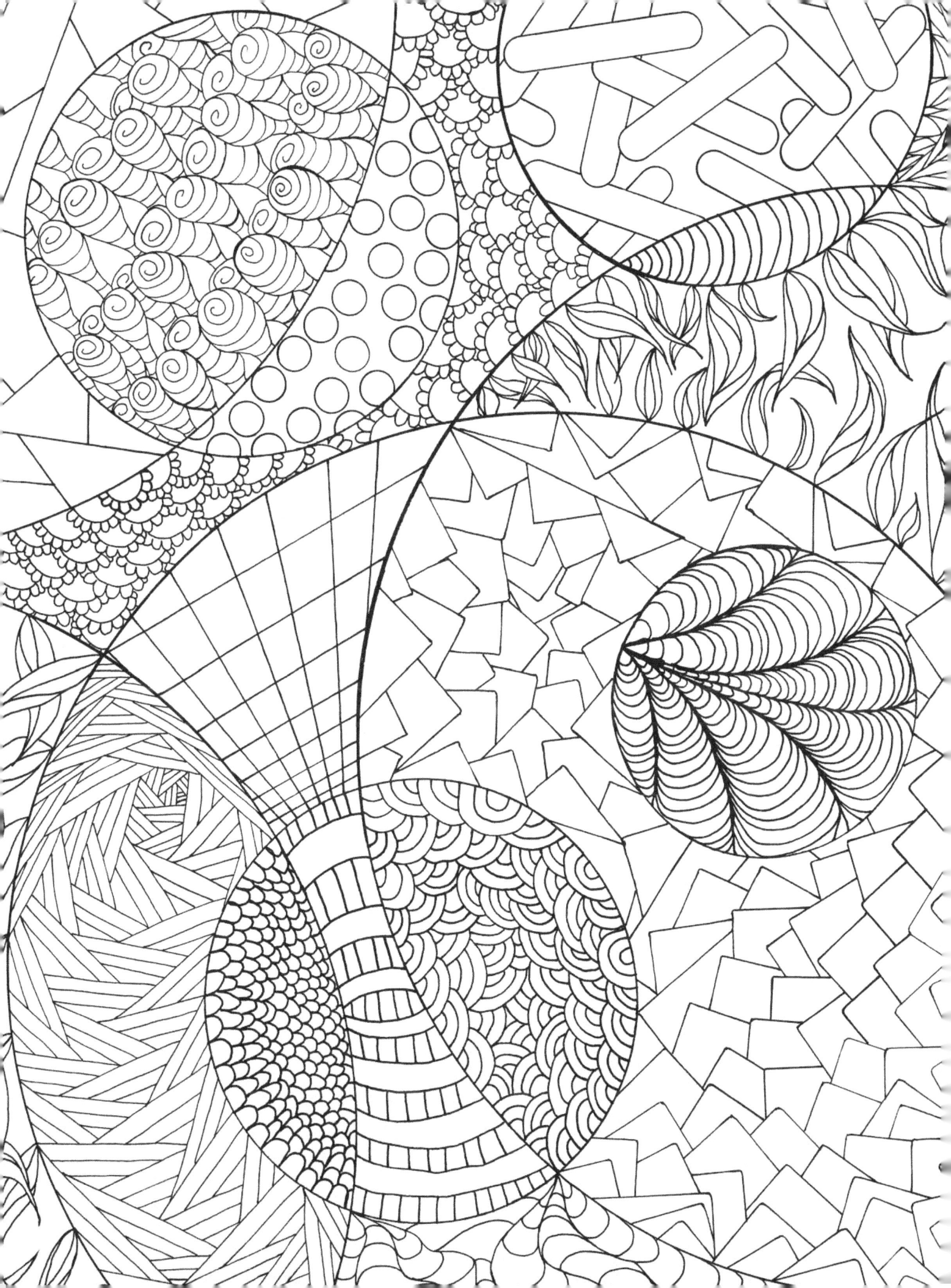

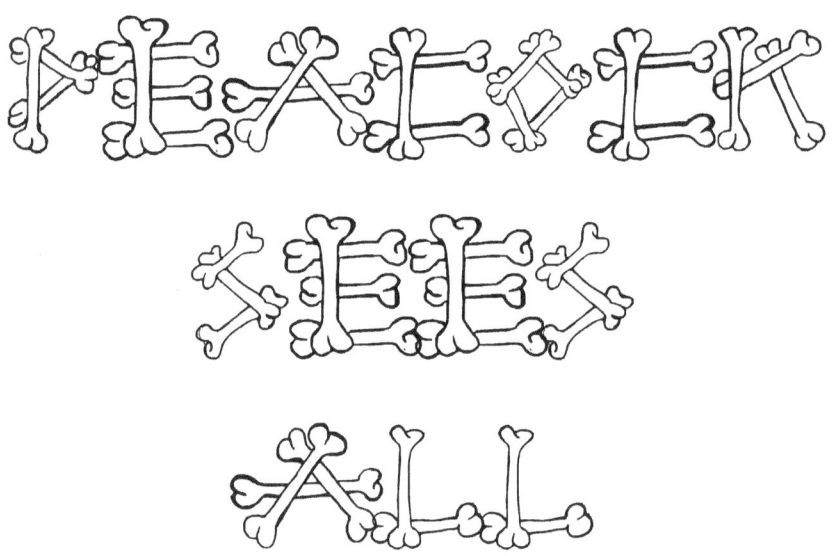

PEACOCK SEES ALL

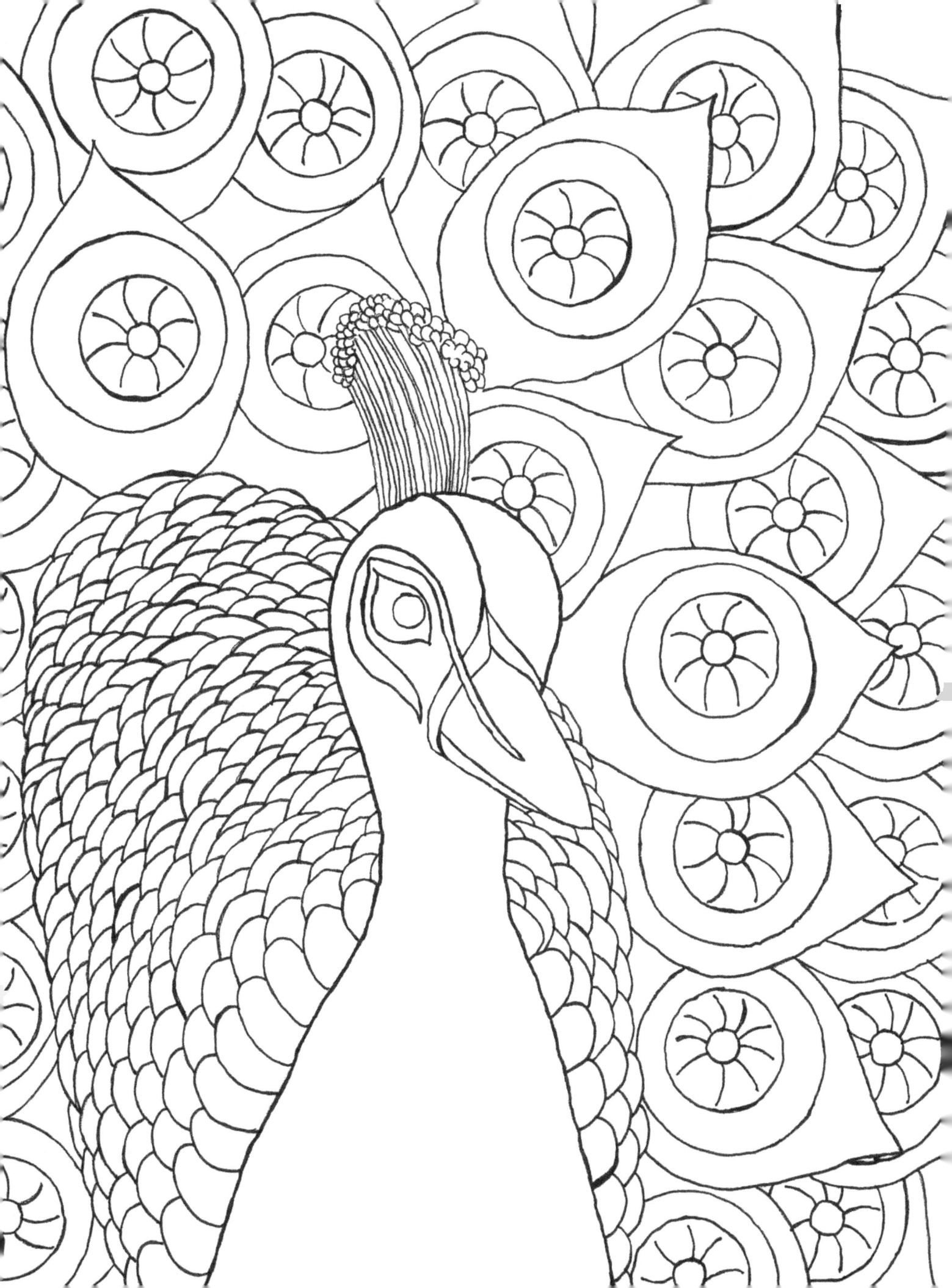

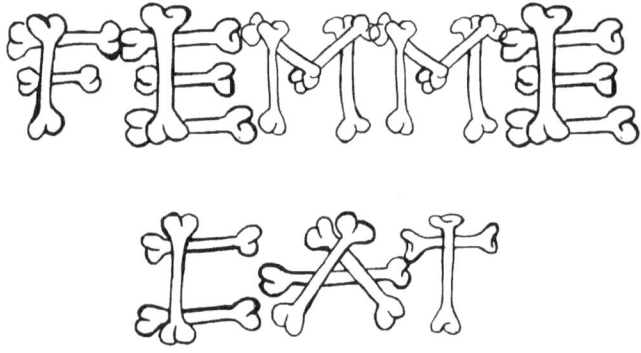

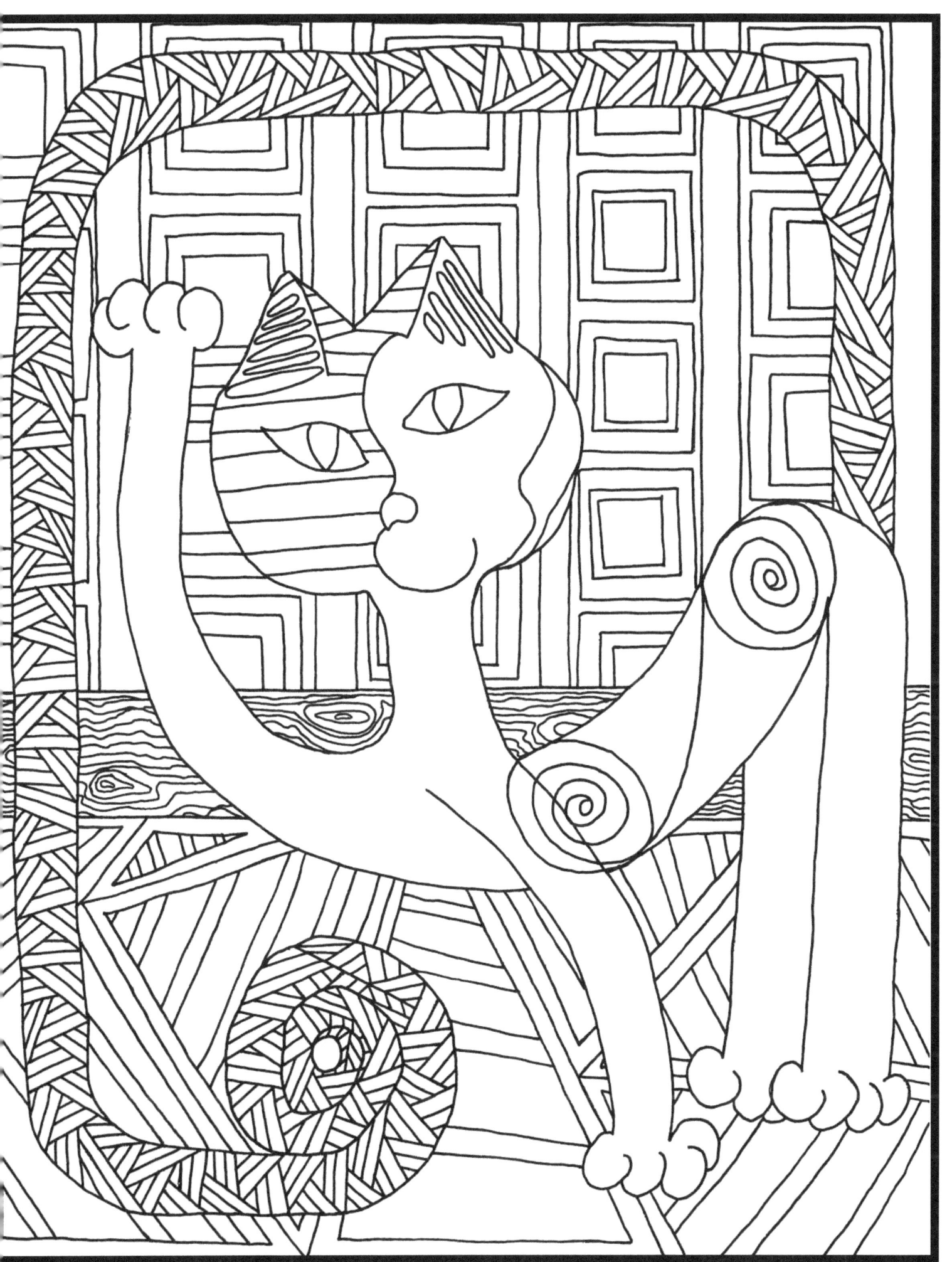

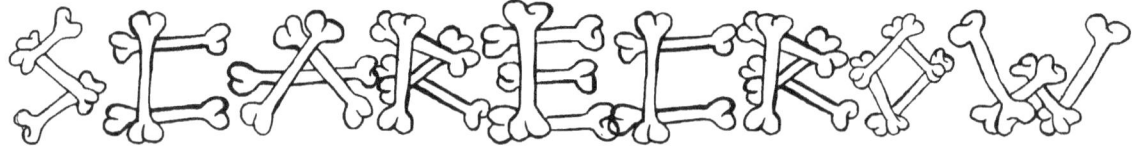

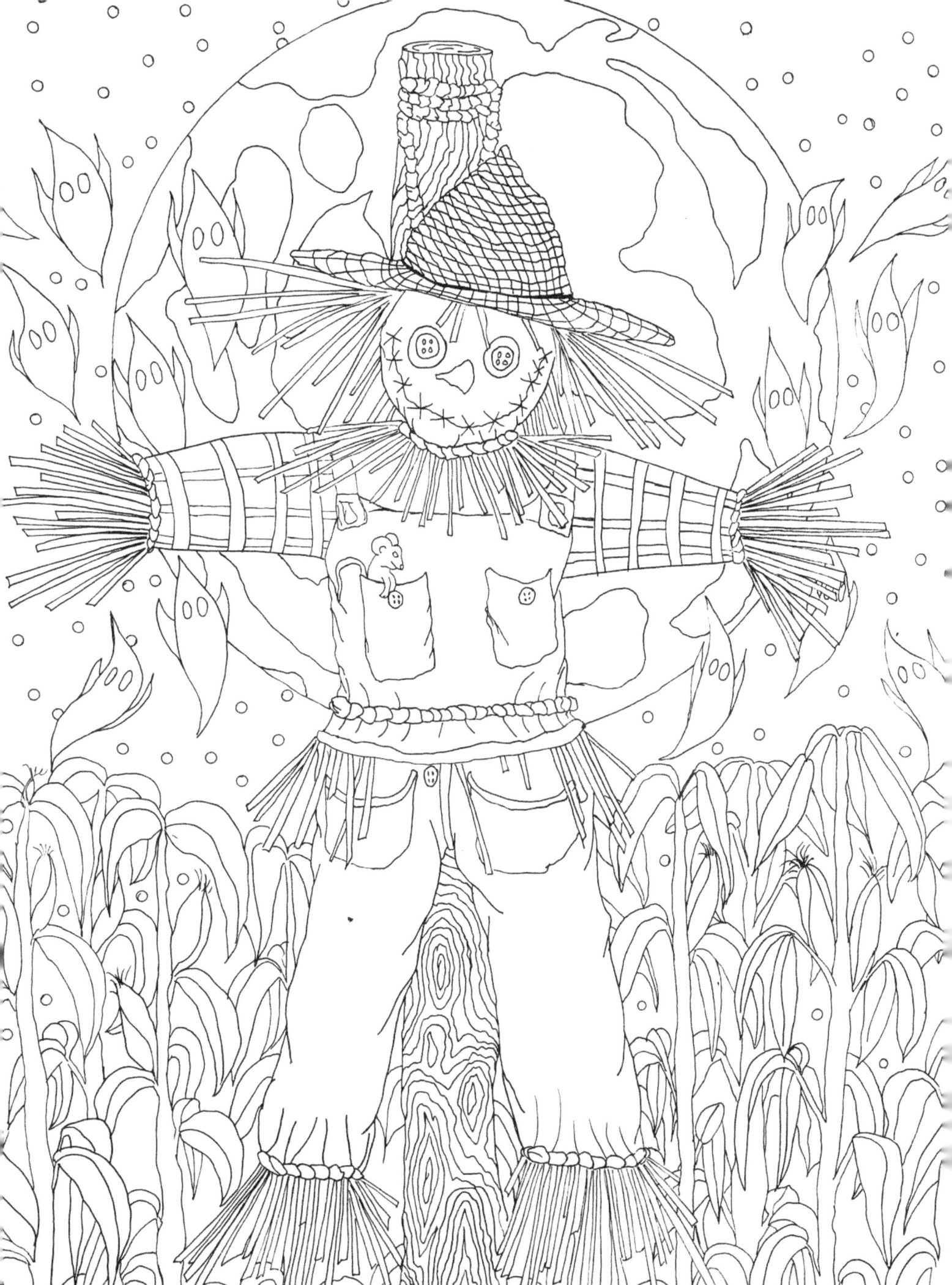

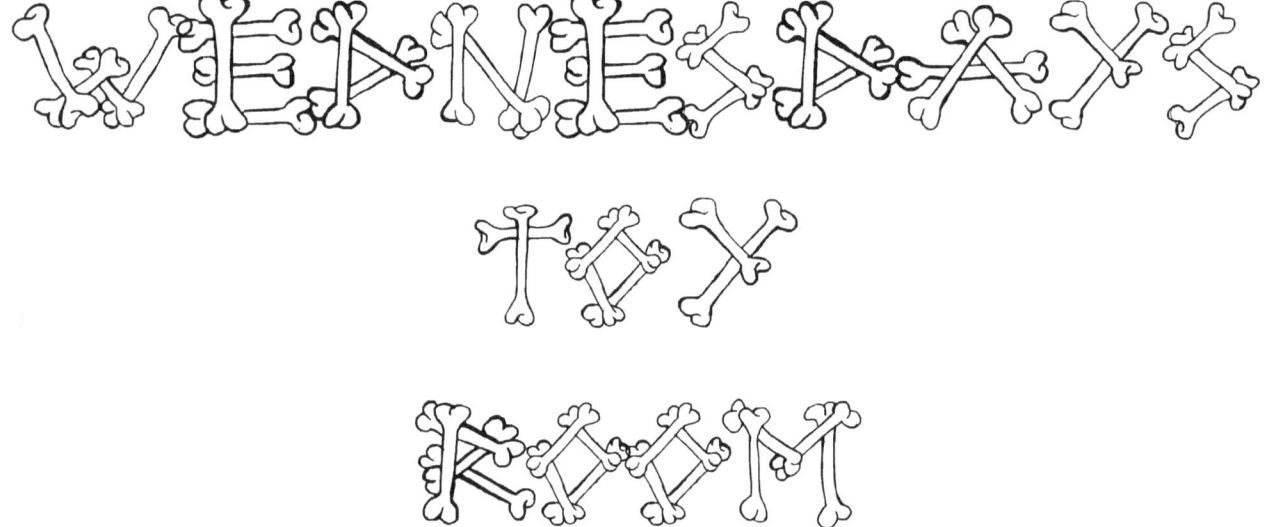

WEDNESDAY'S
TOY
ROOM

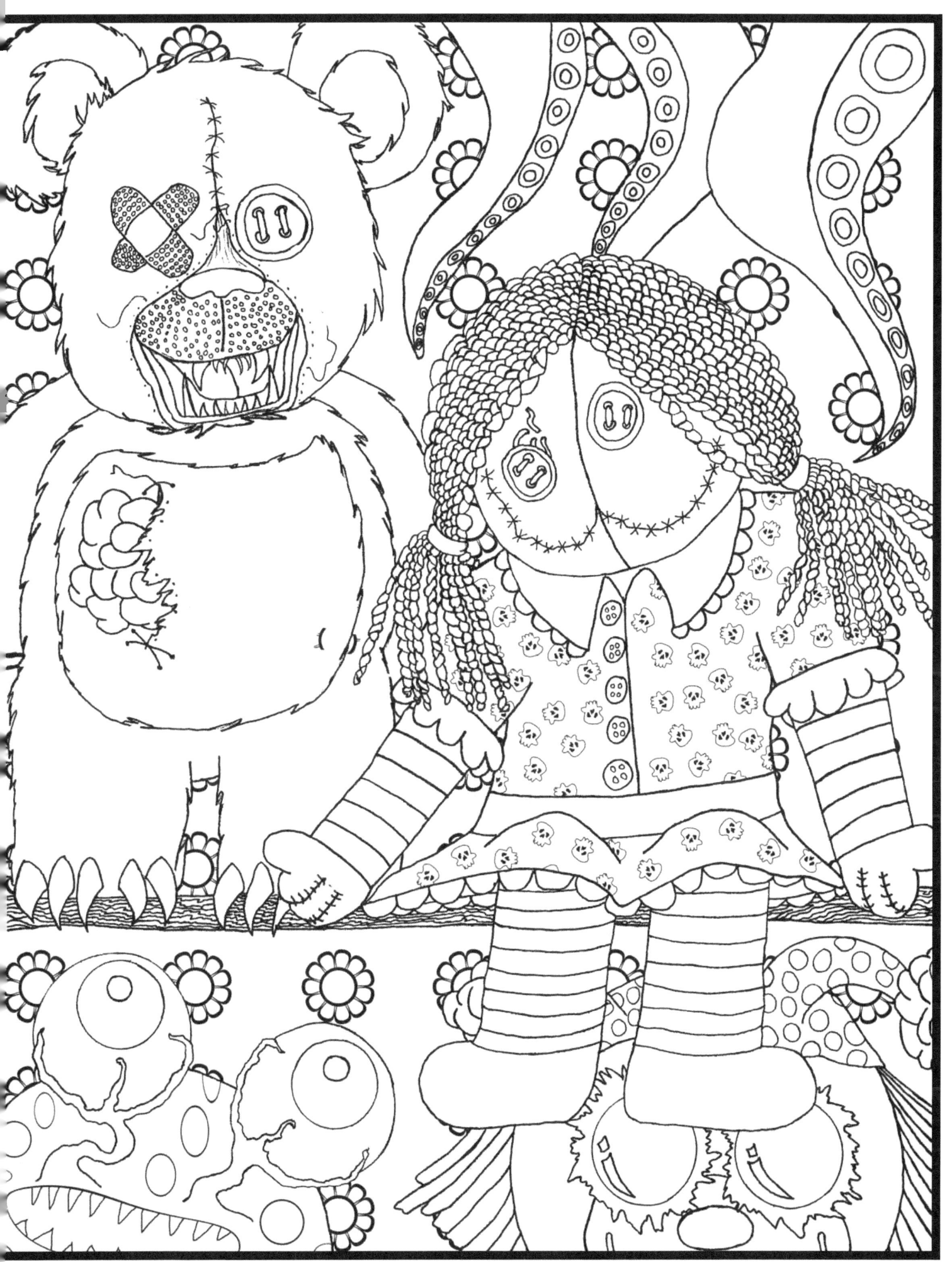

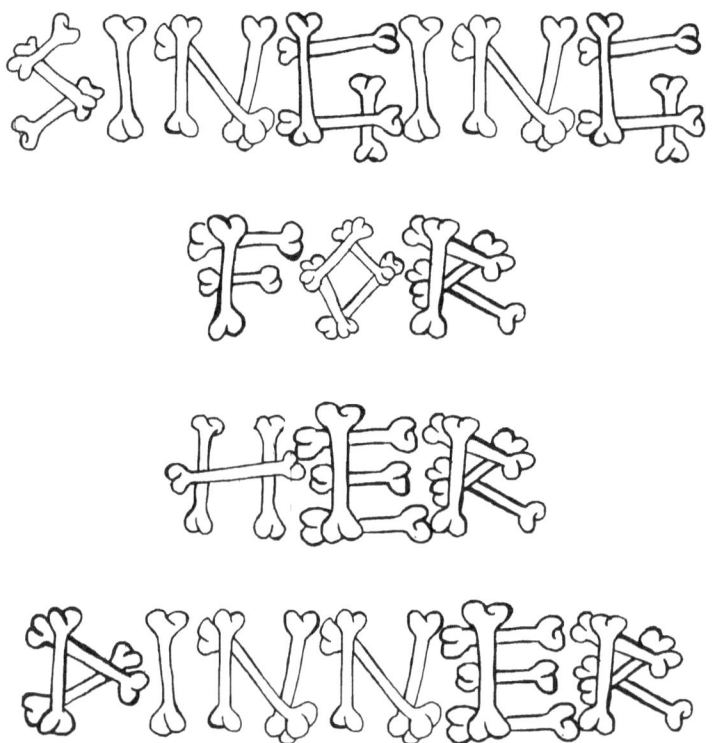

SINGING
FOR
HER
DINNER

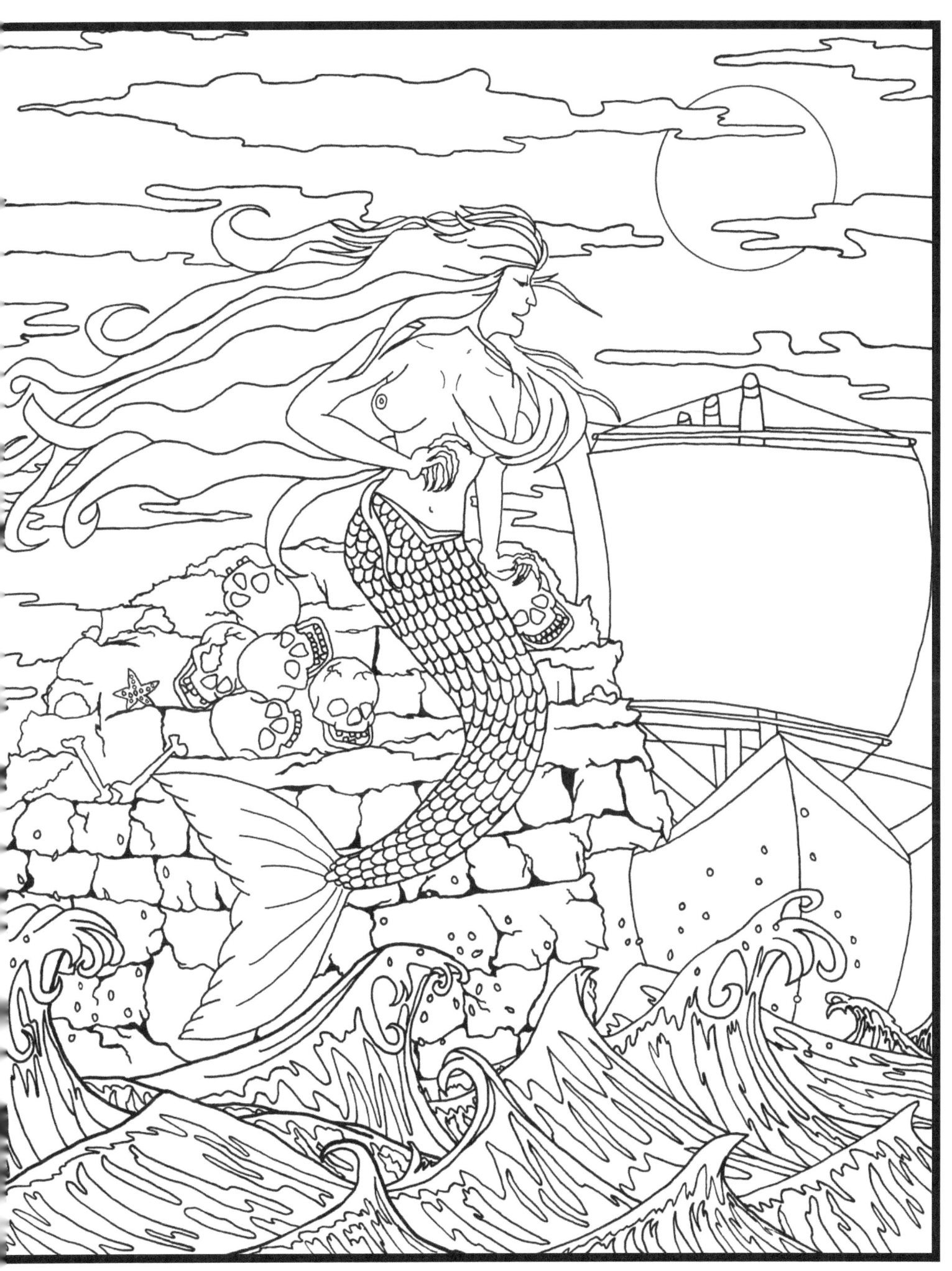

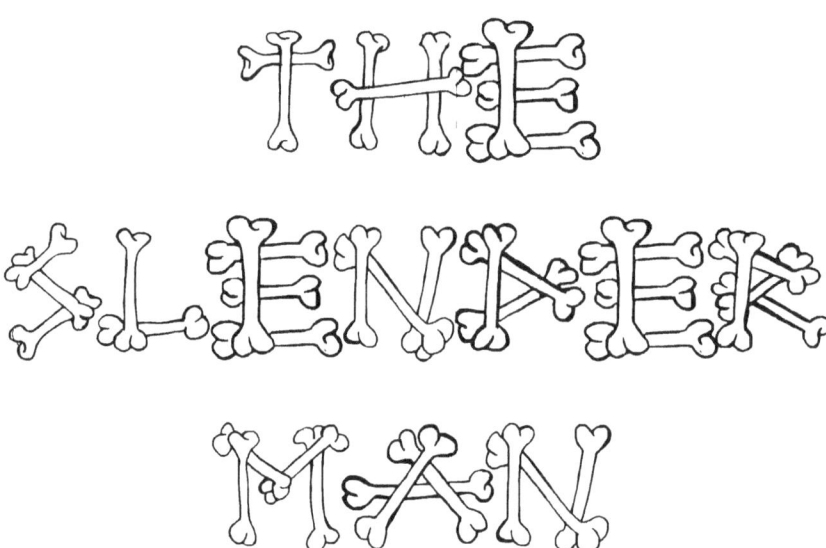

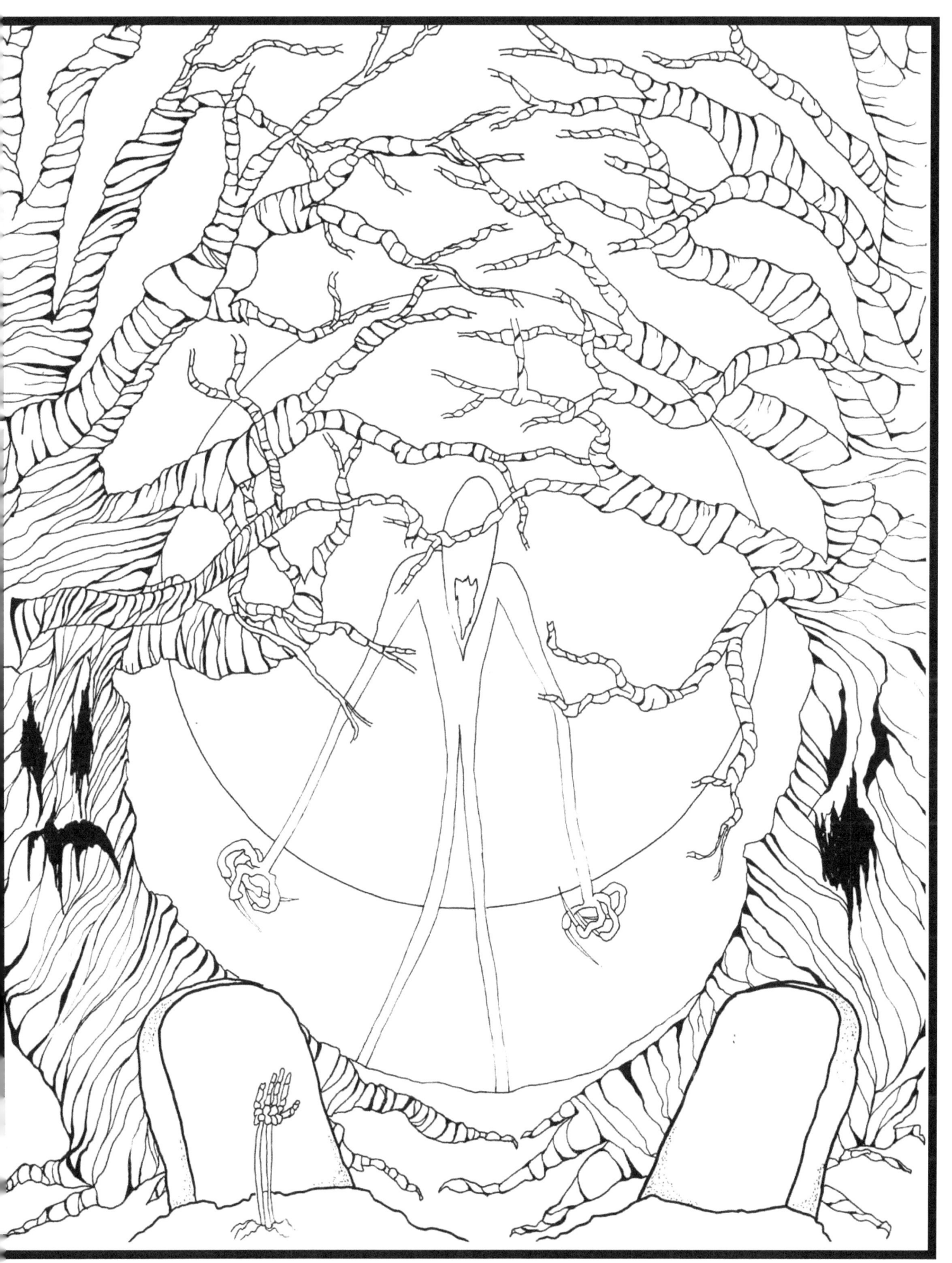

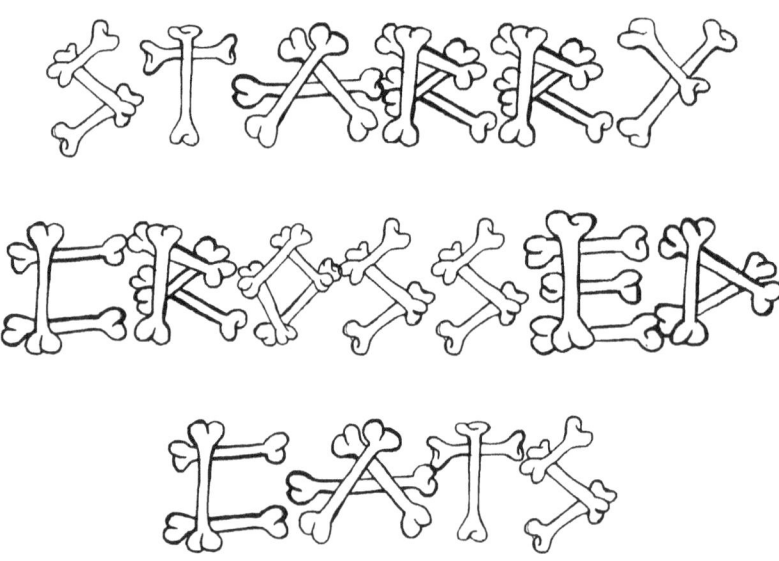

STARRY CROSSED CATS

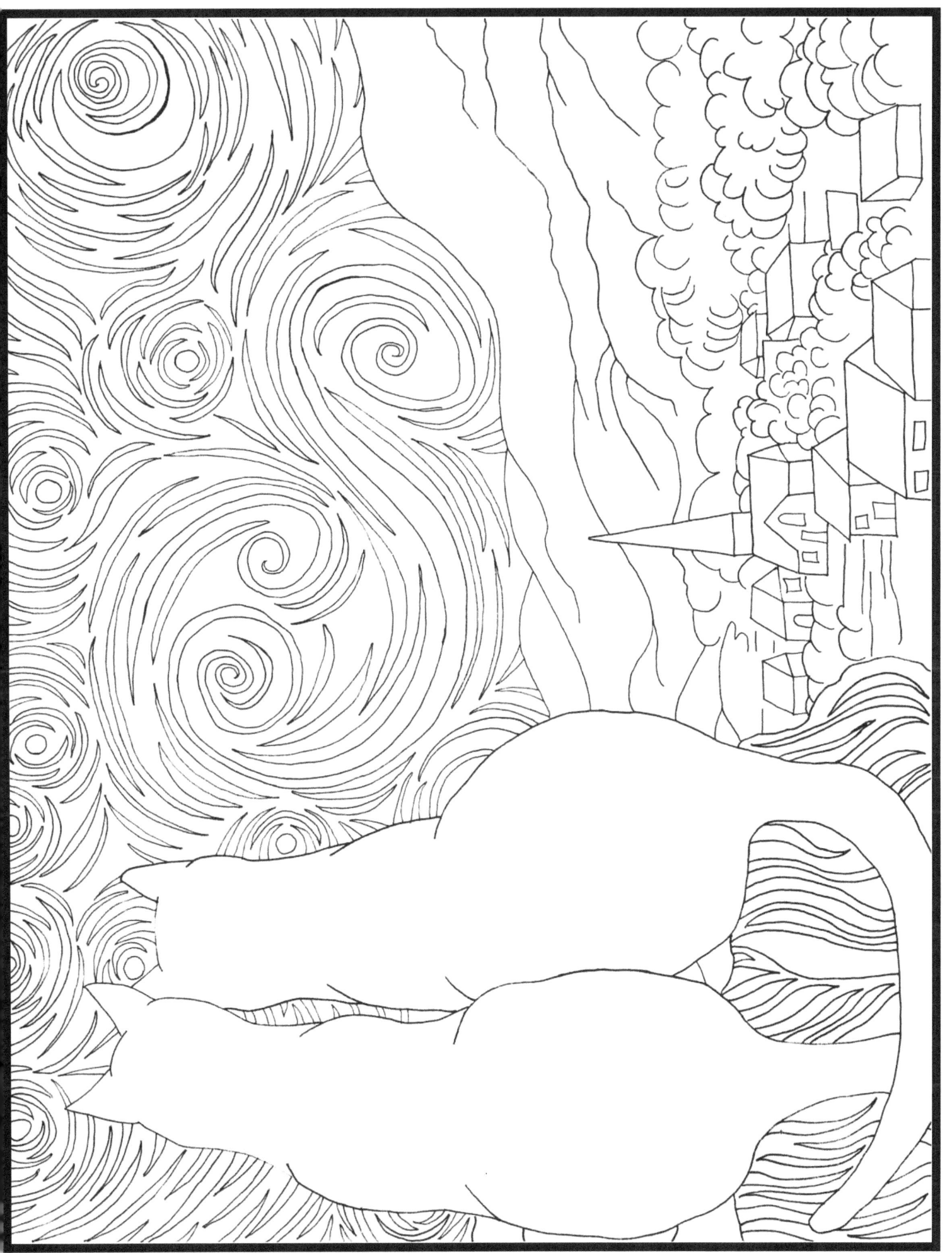

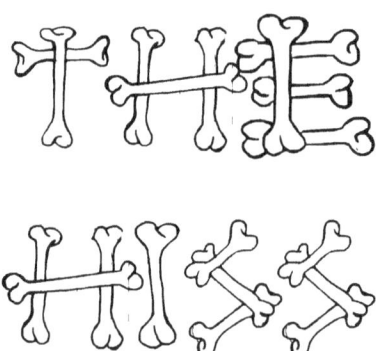

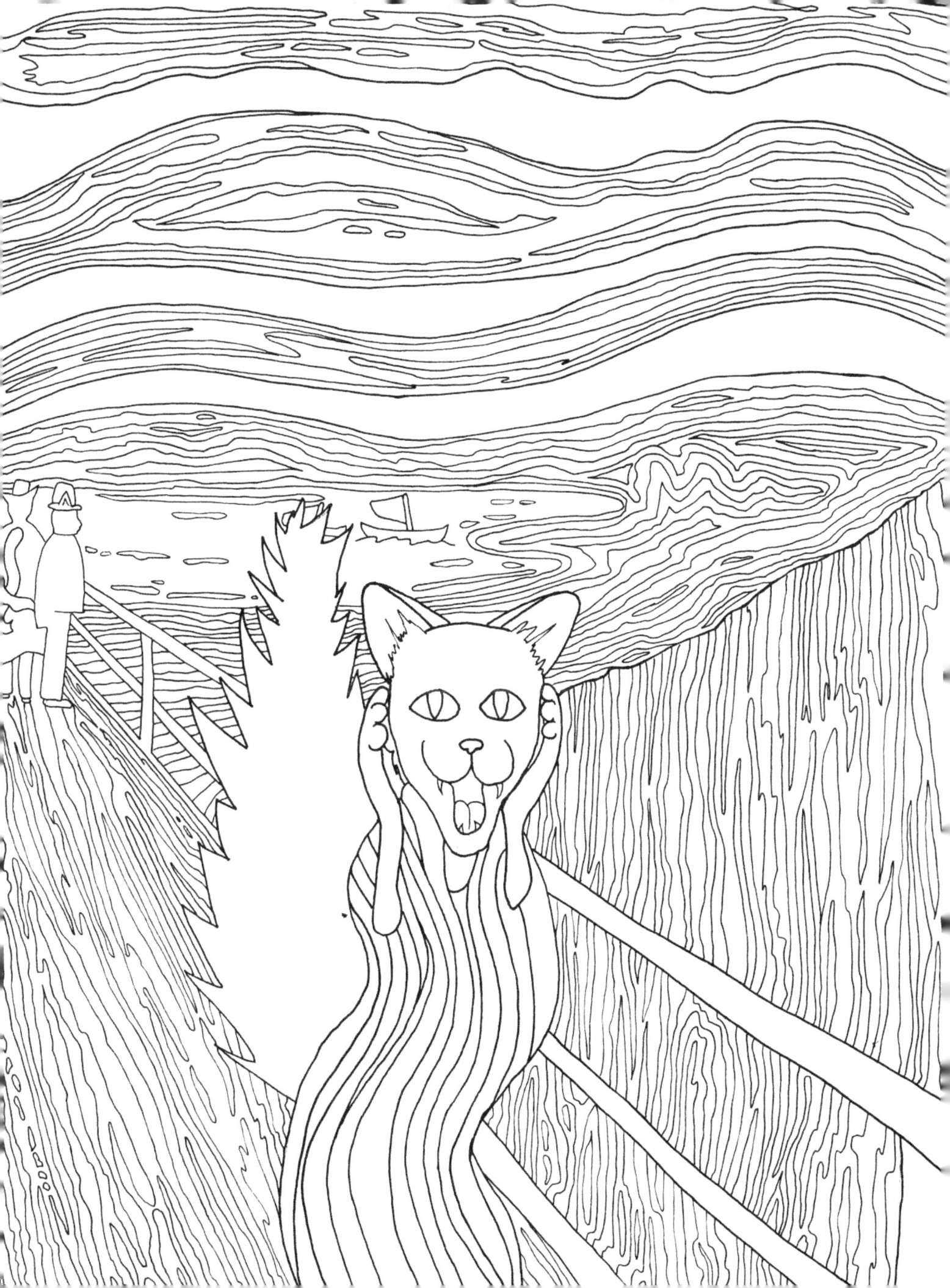

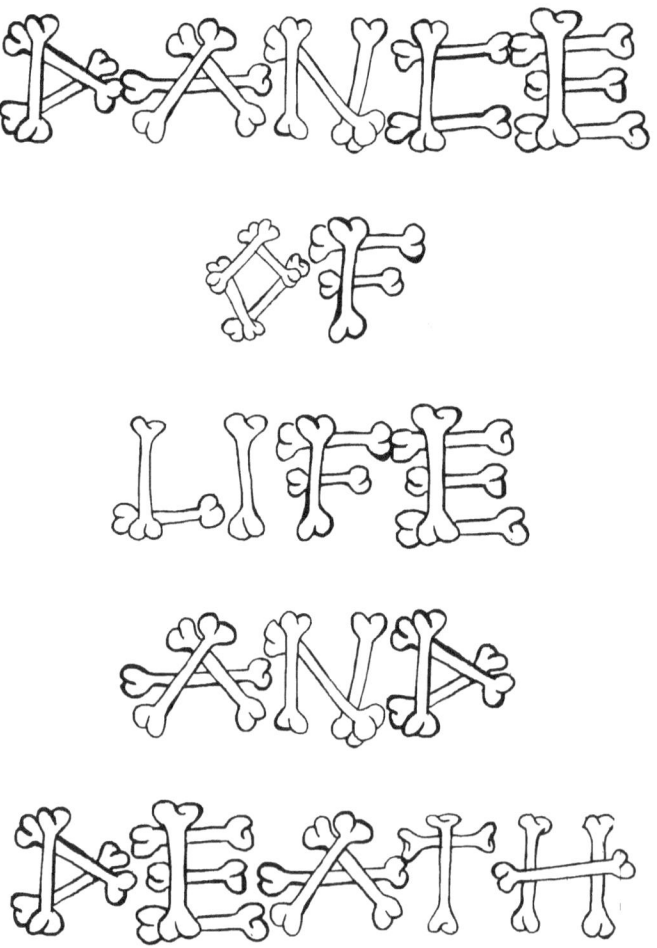

DANCE
OF
LIFE
AND
DEATH

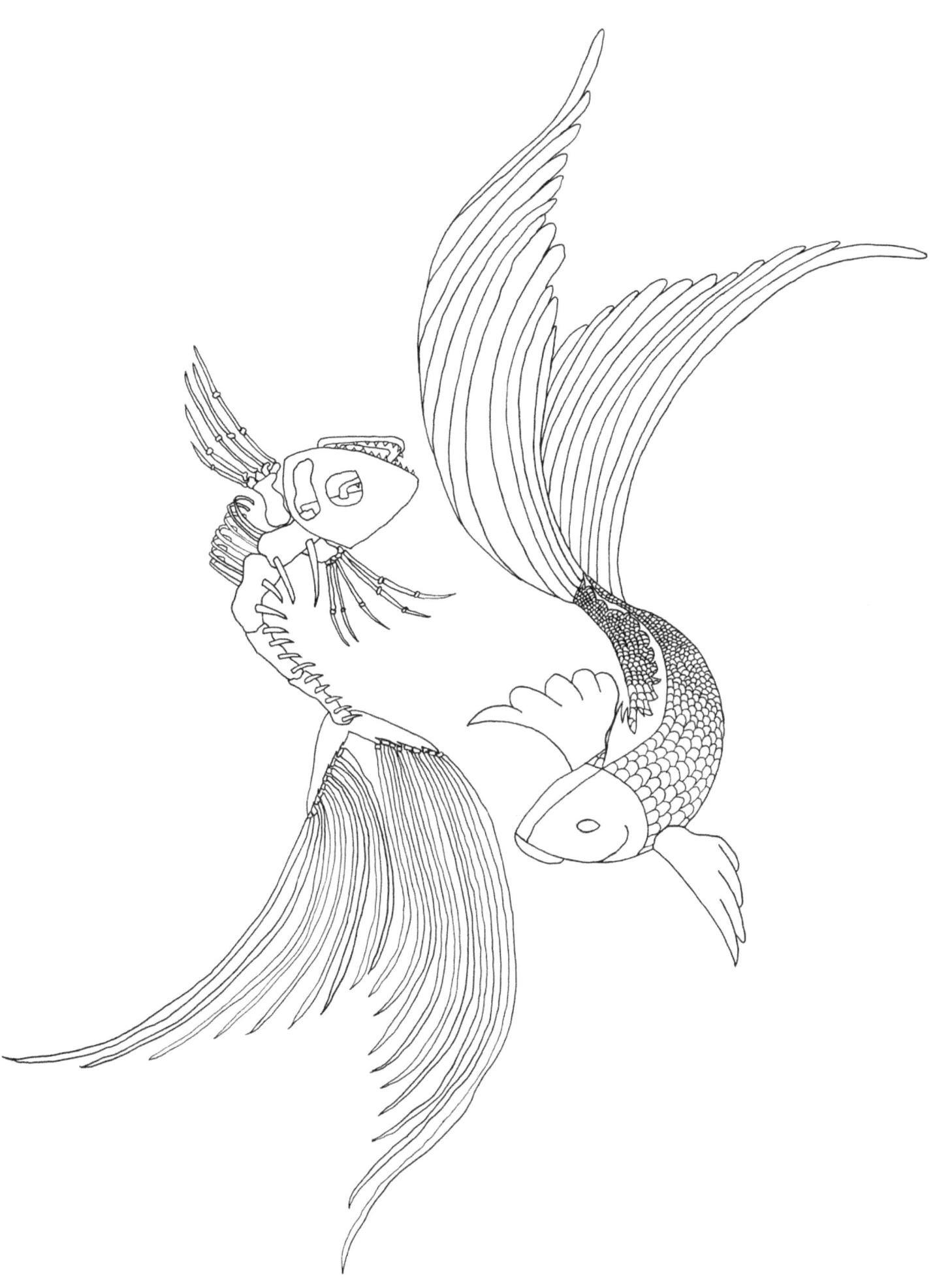

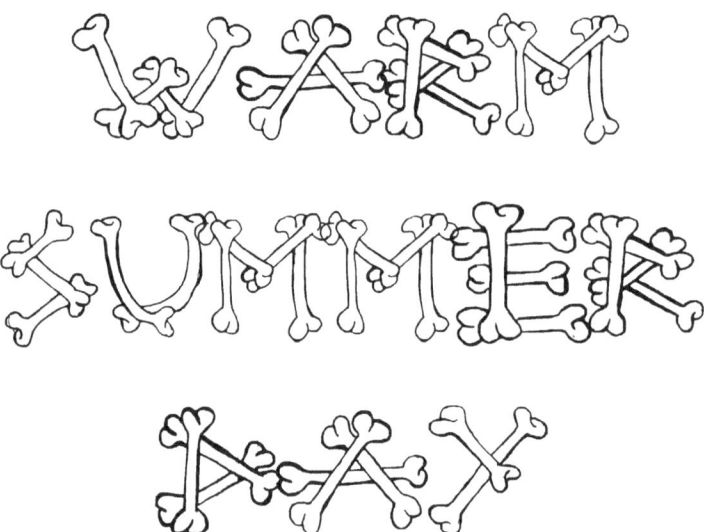

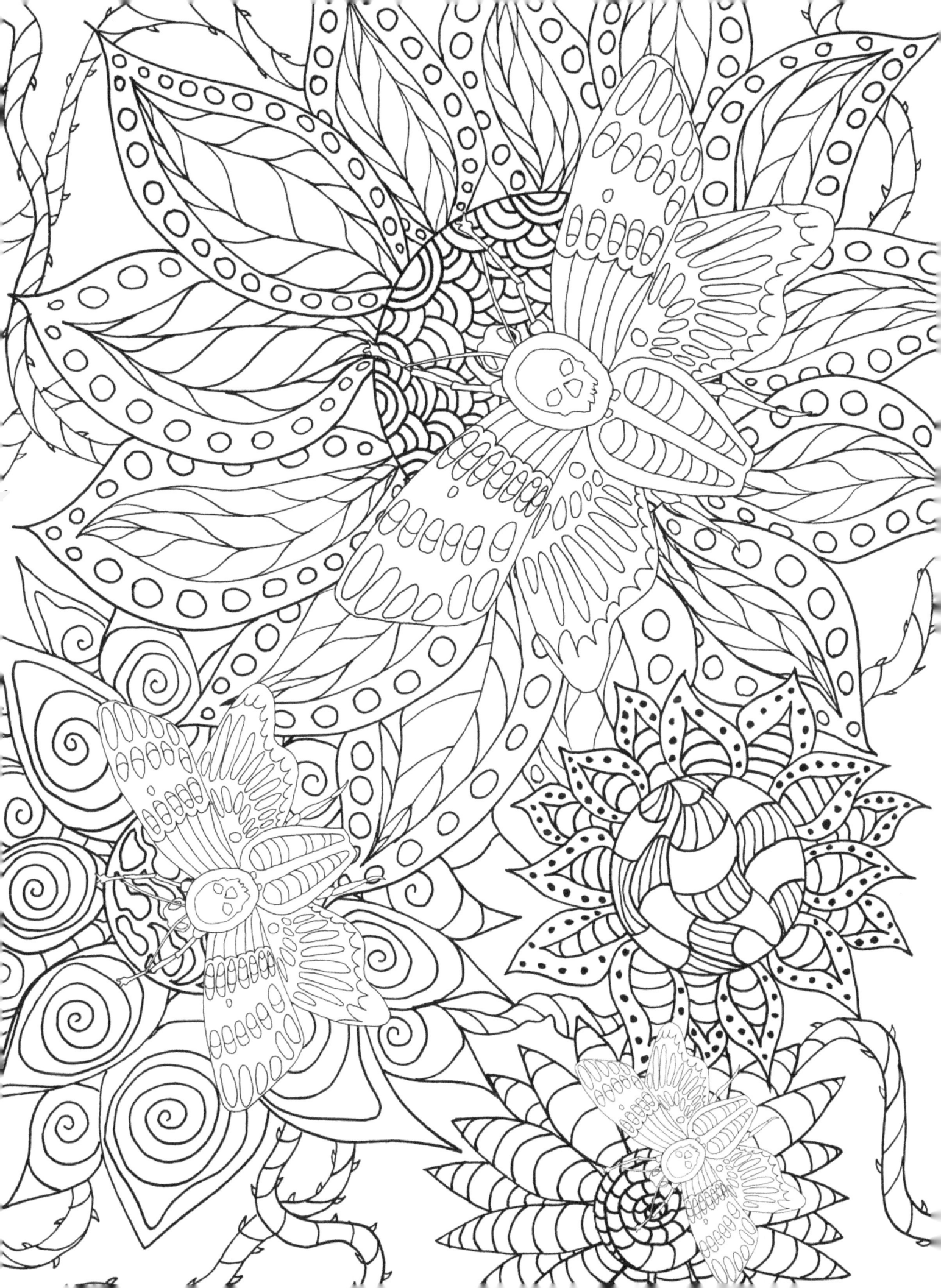

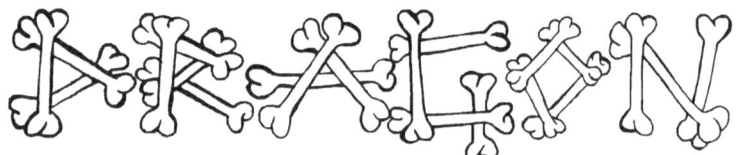

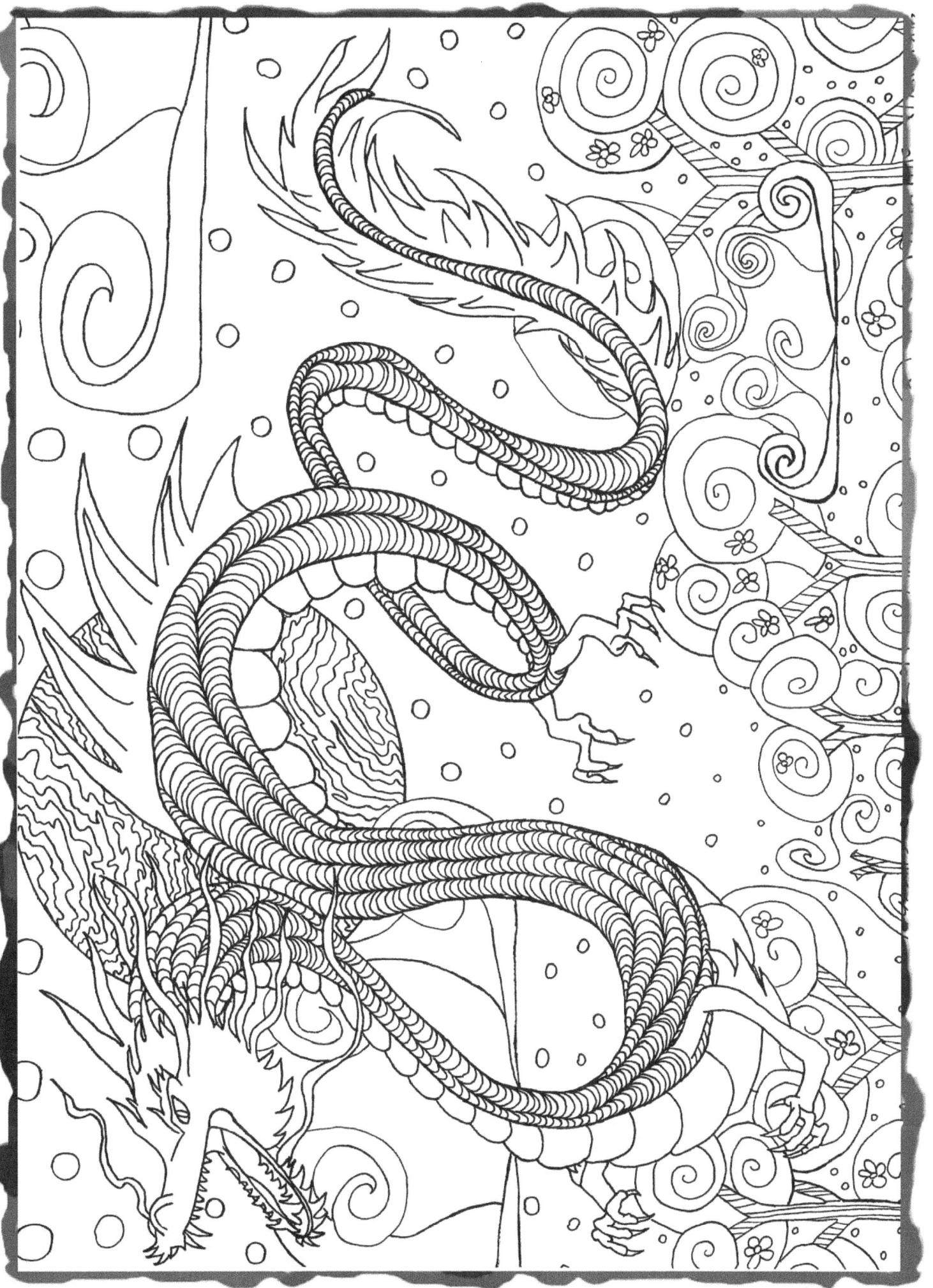

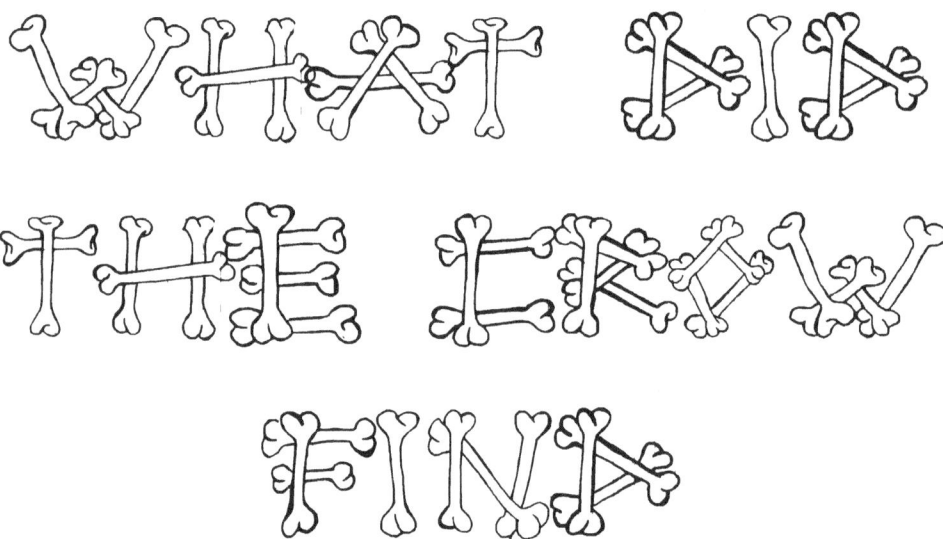

WHAT DID
THE CROW
FIND

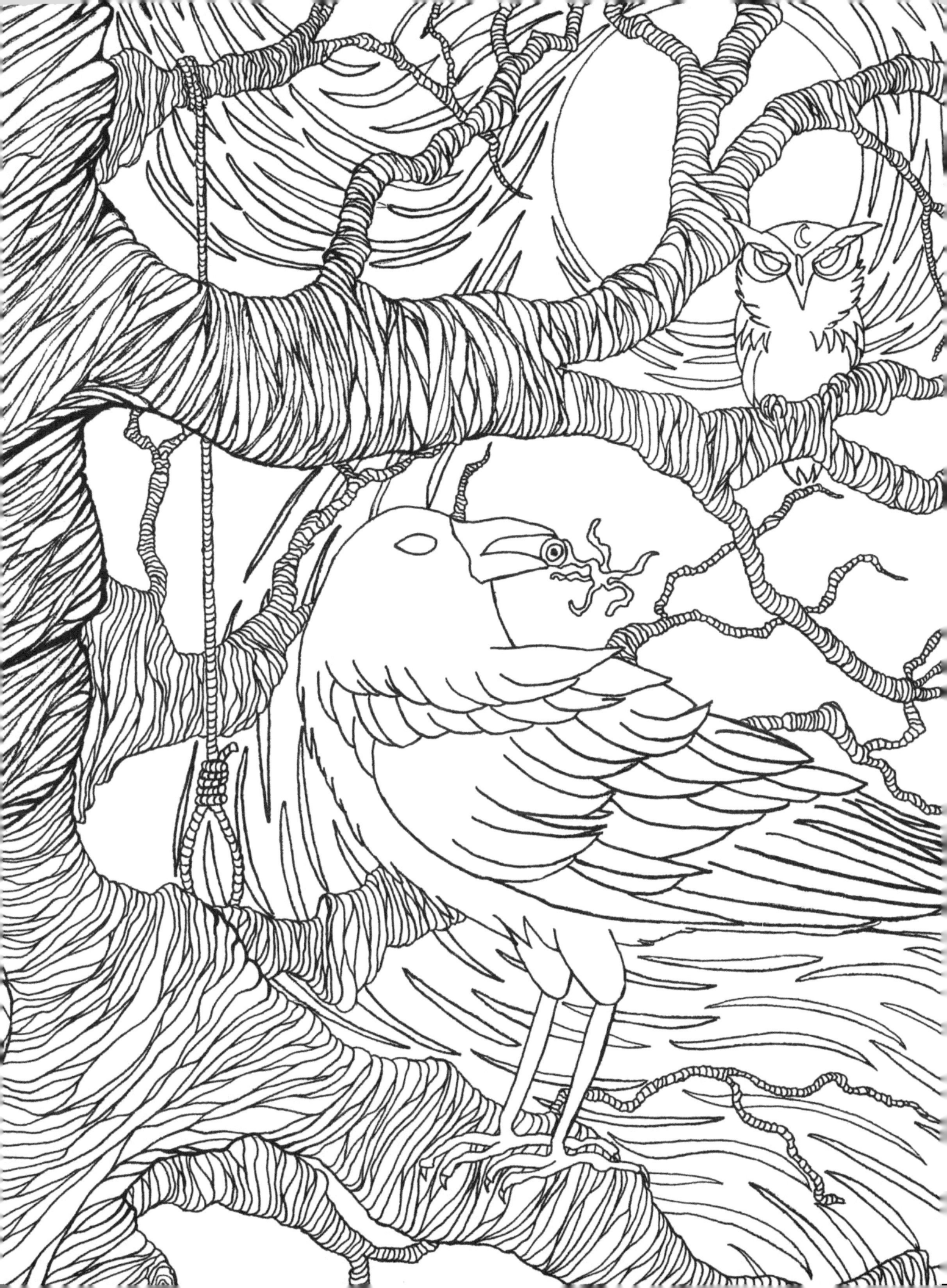

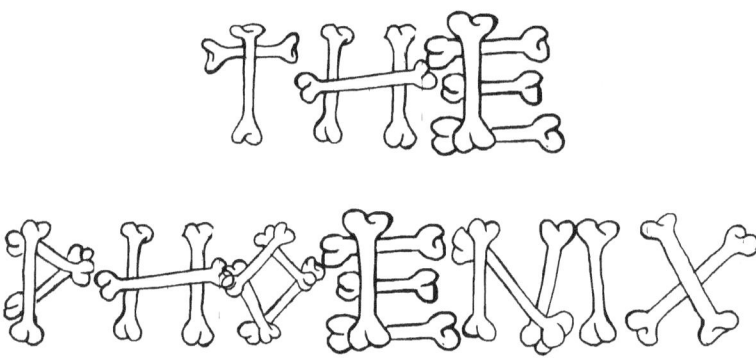

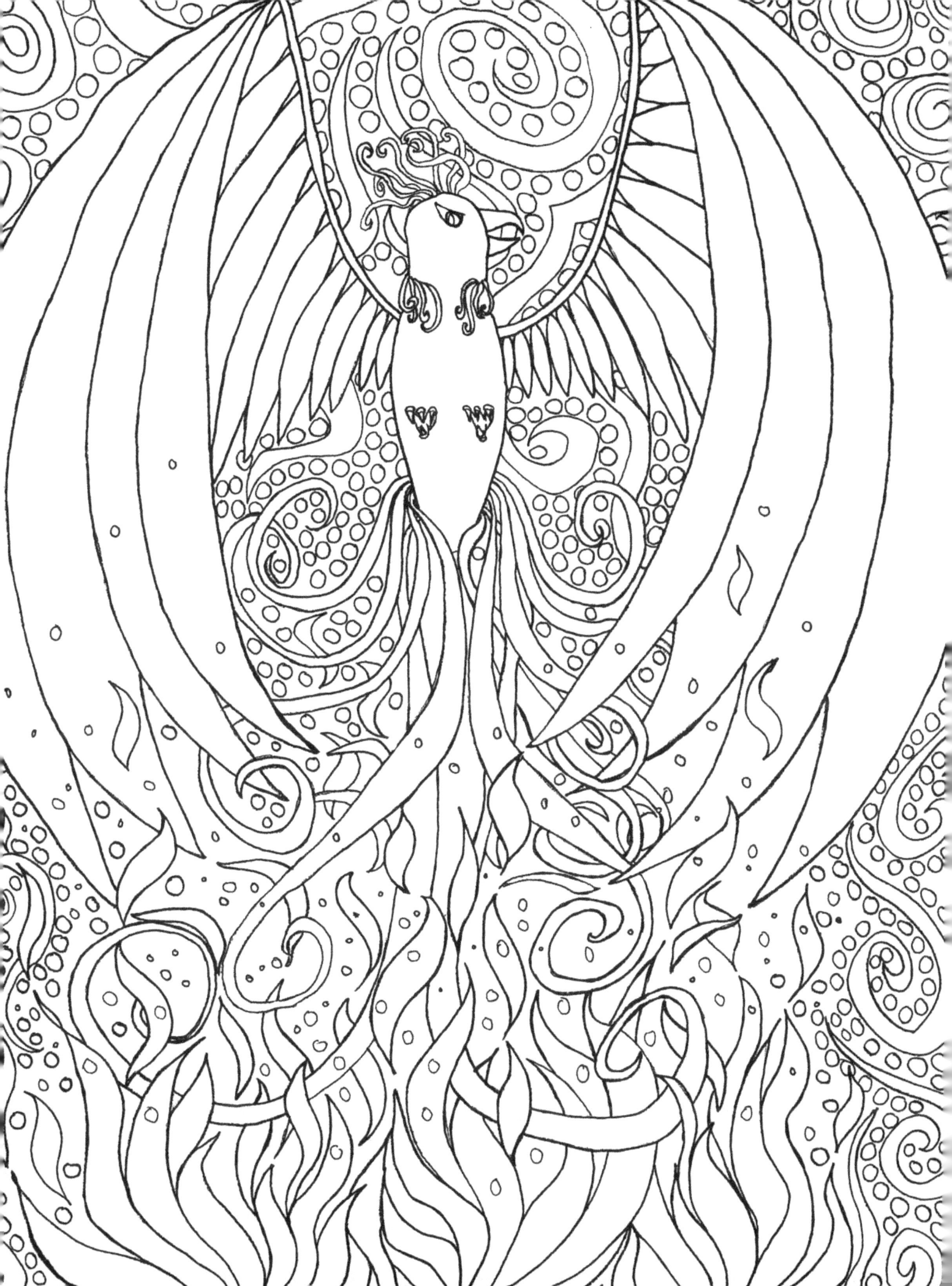

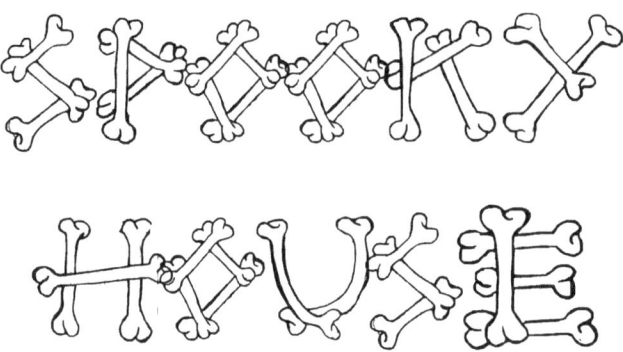

SPOOKY HOUSE

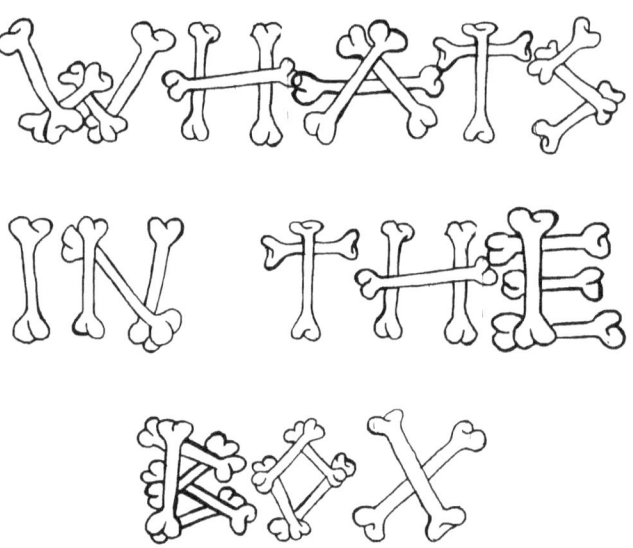

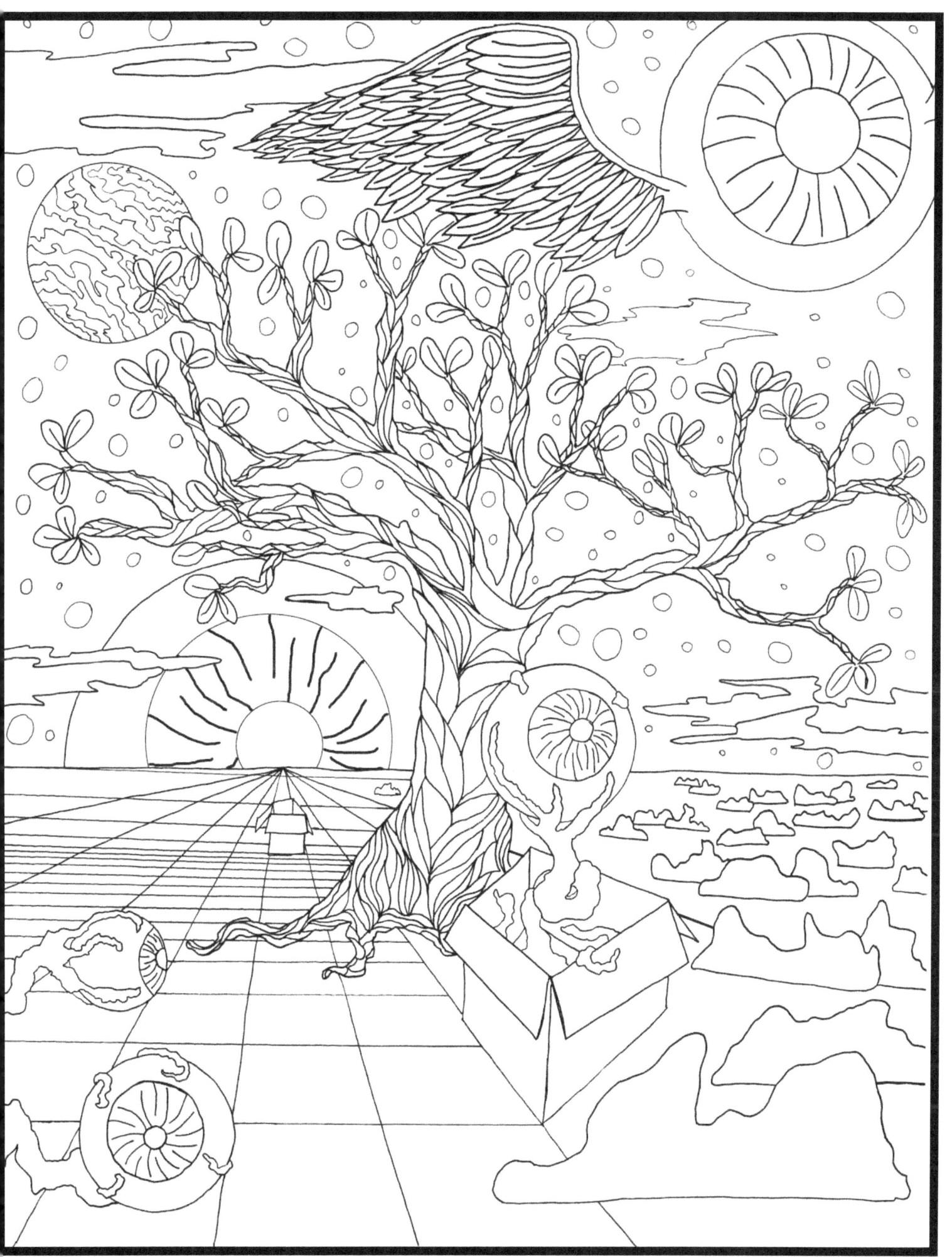

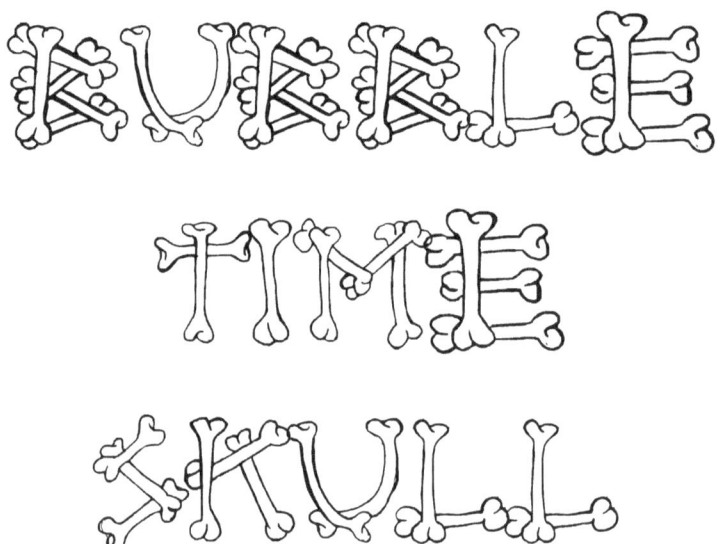

BUBBLE TIME SKULL

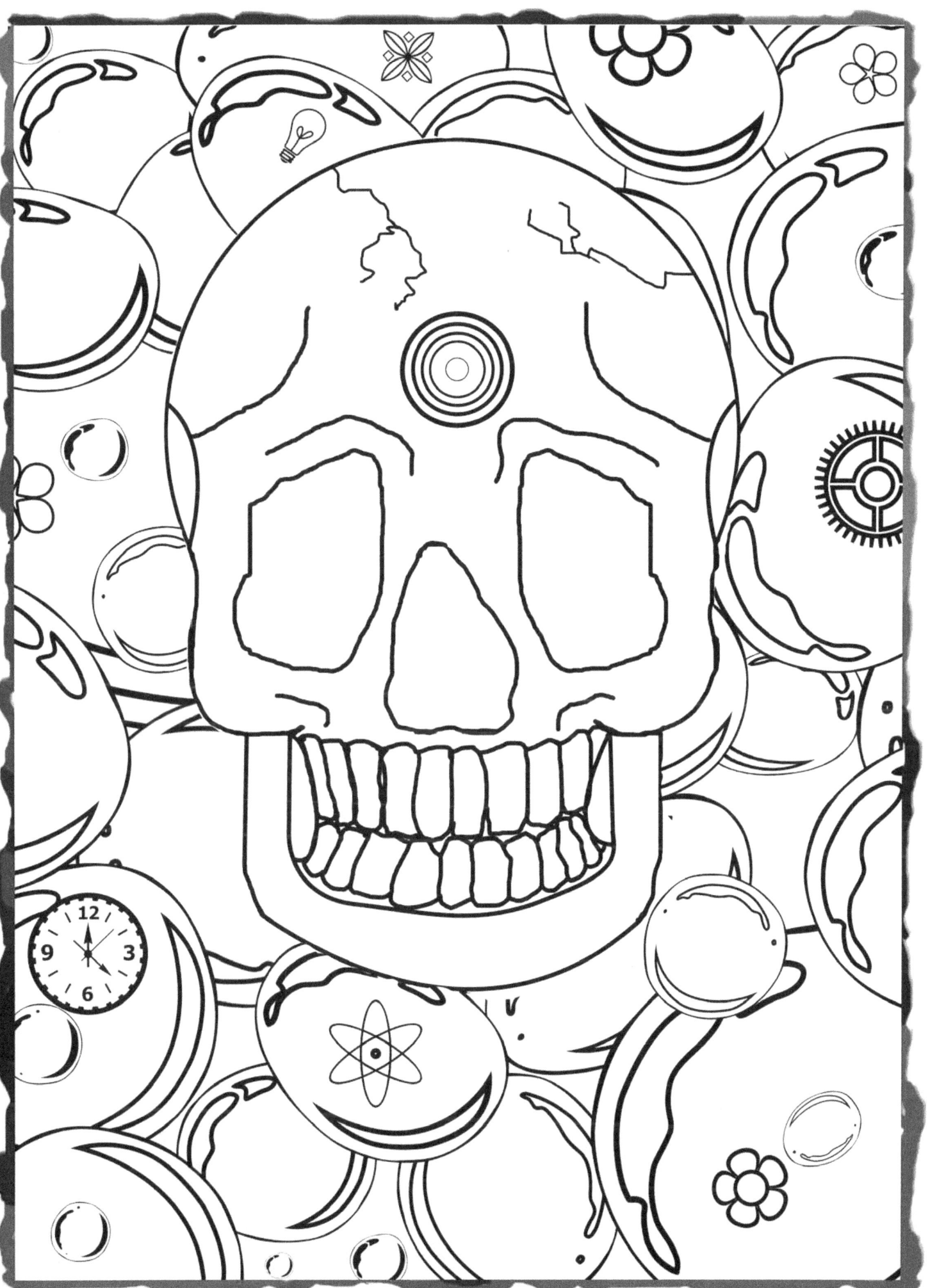

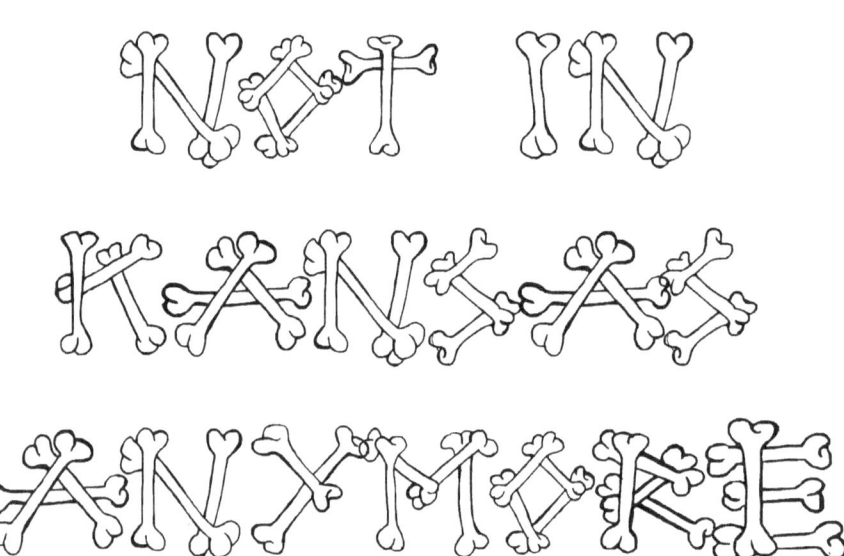

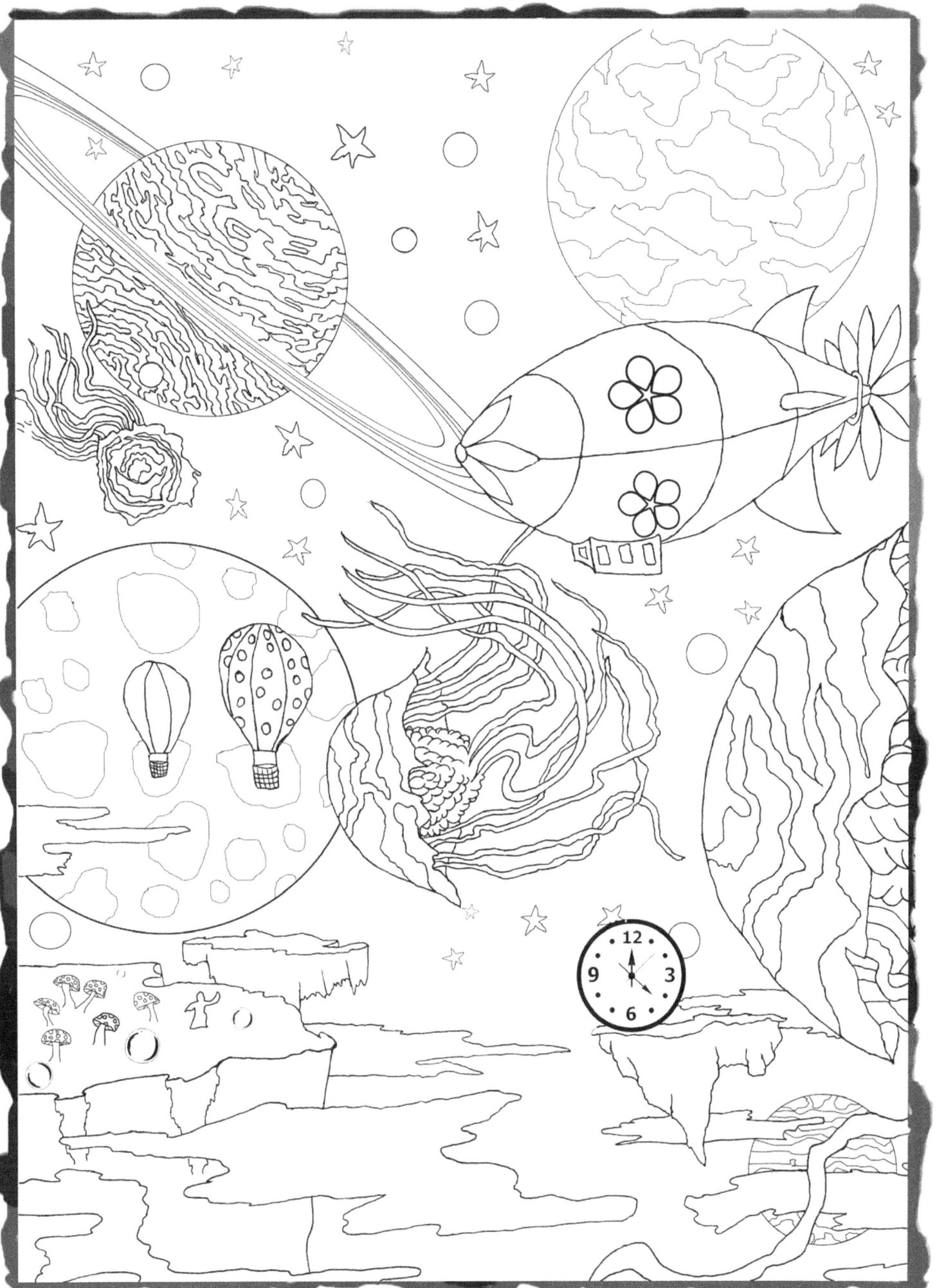

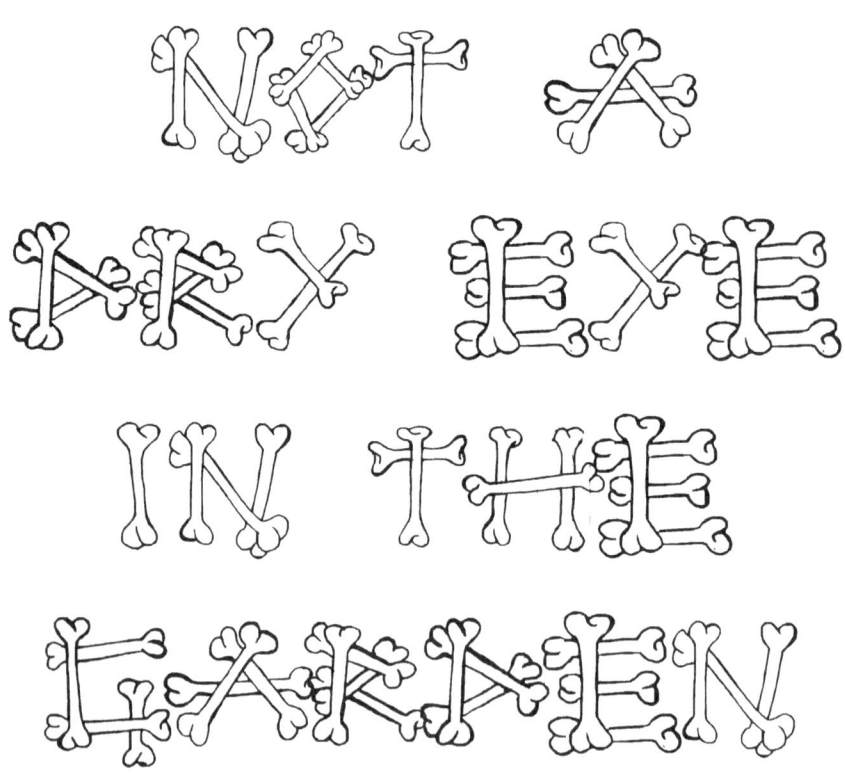

NOT A
DRY EYE
IN THE
GARDEN

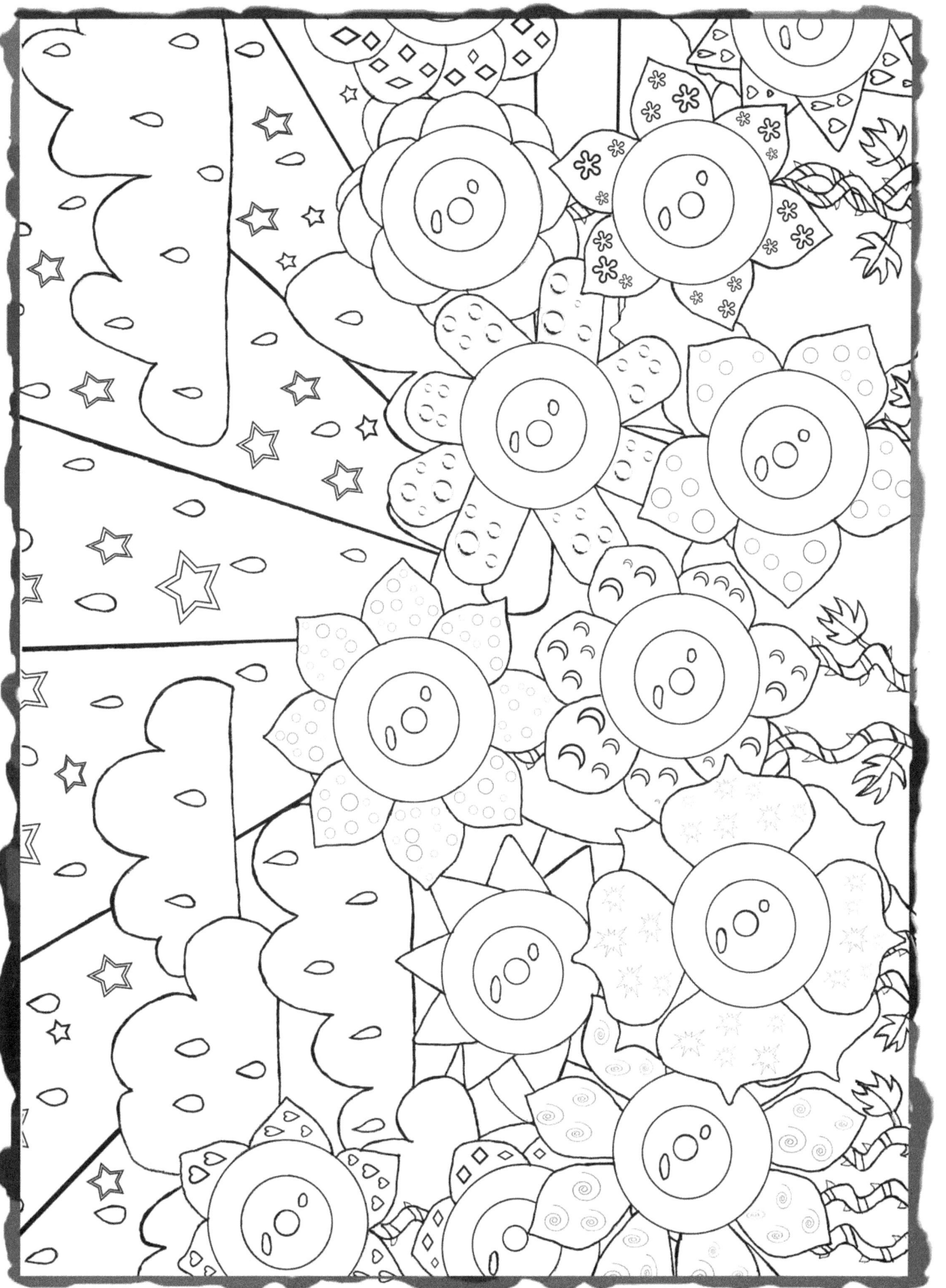

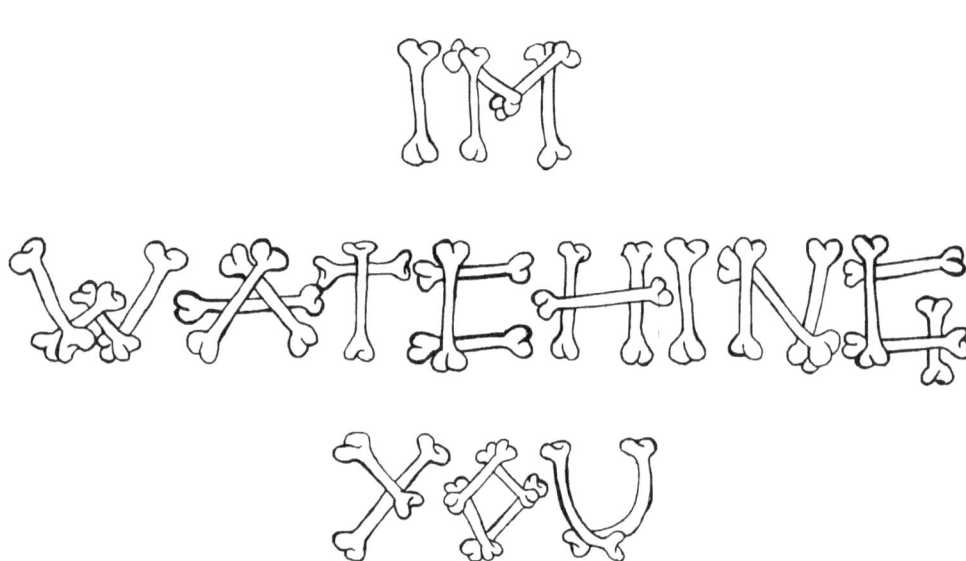

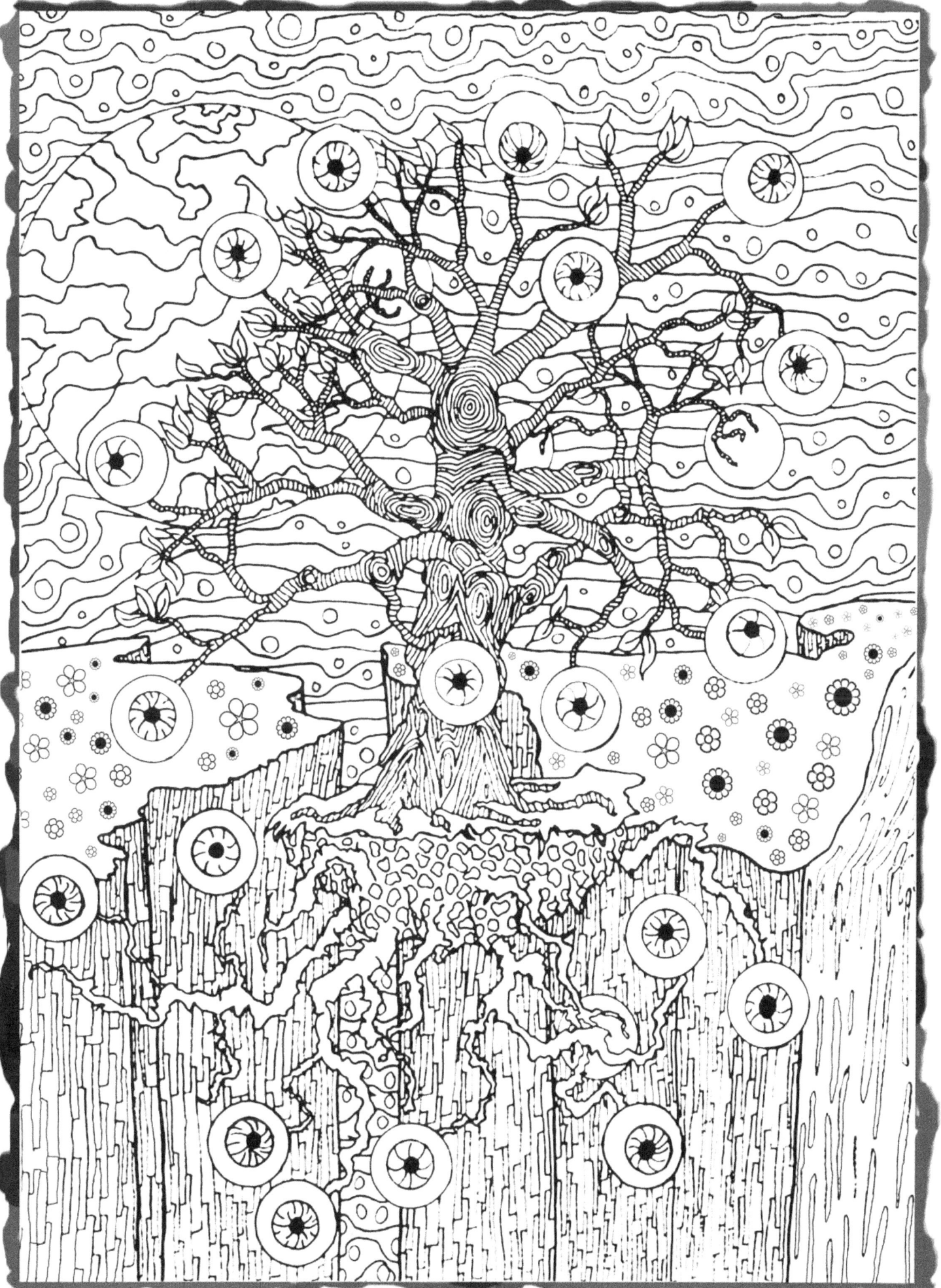

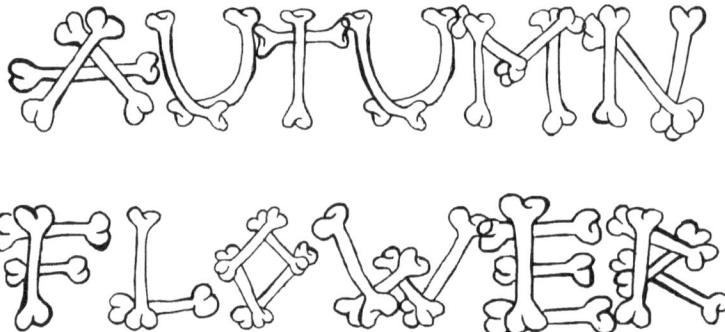

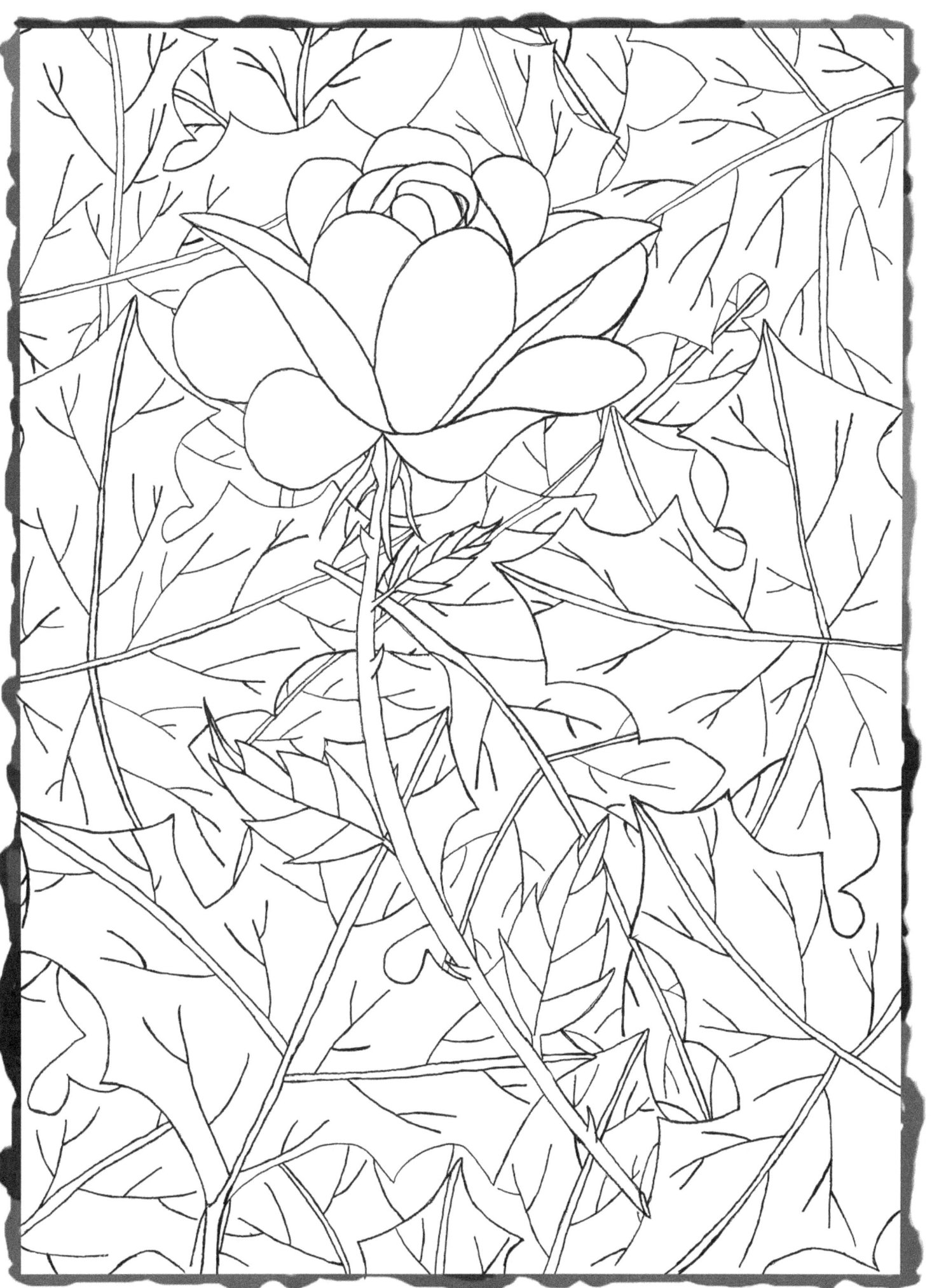

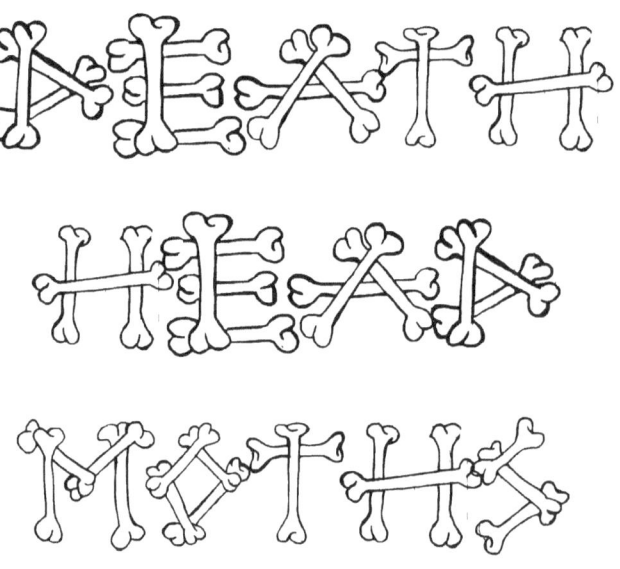

DEATH HEAD MOTHS

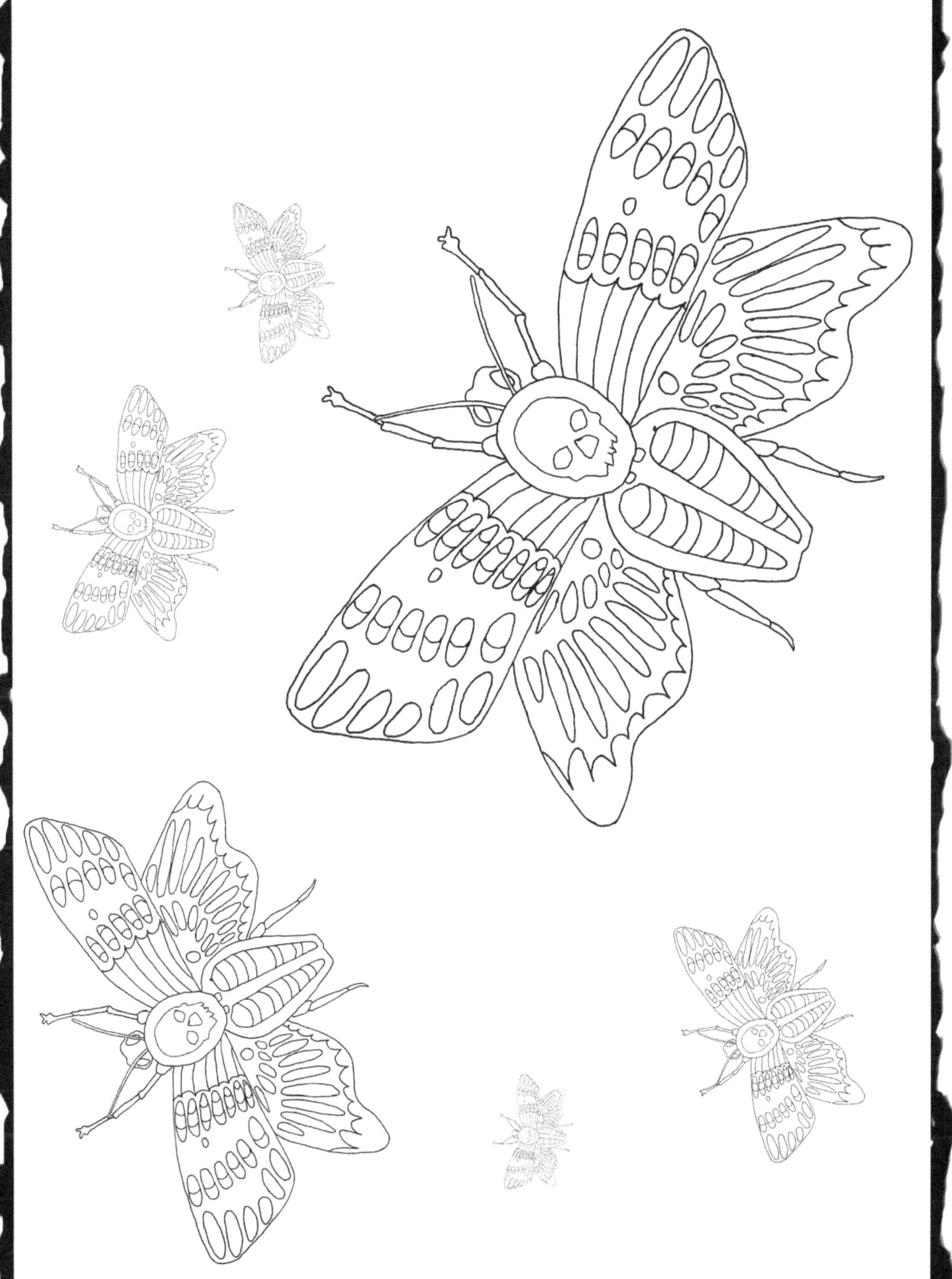

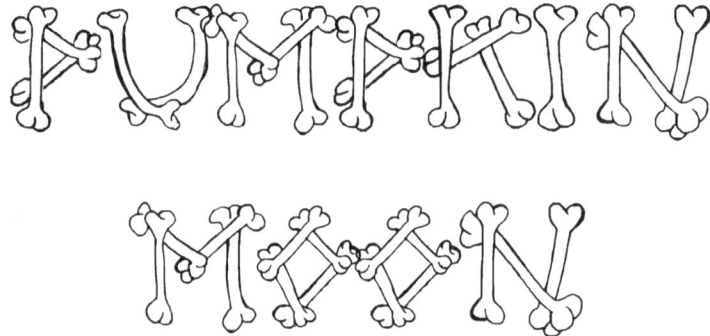

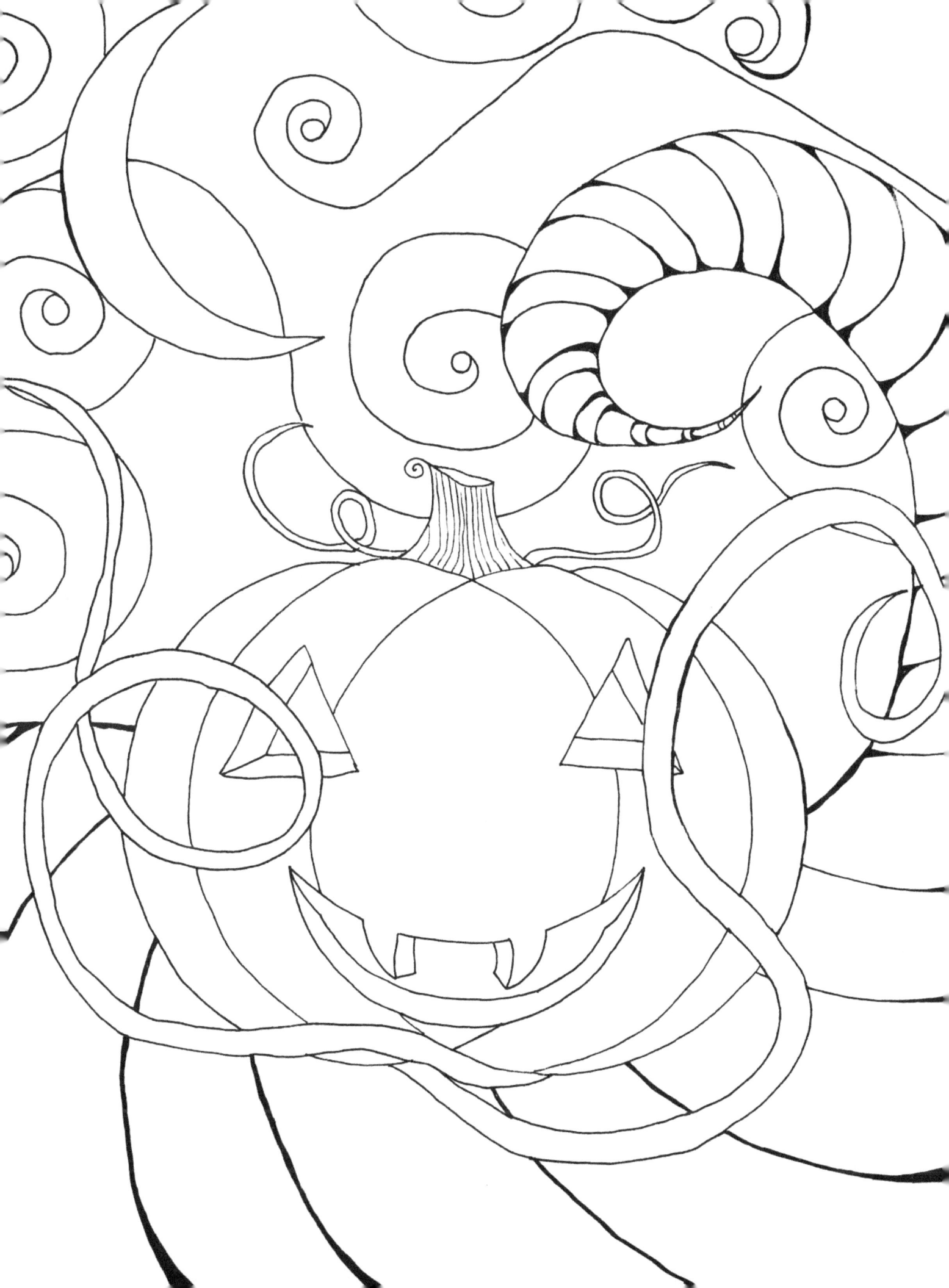

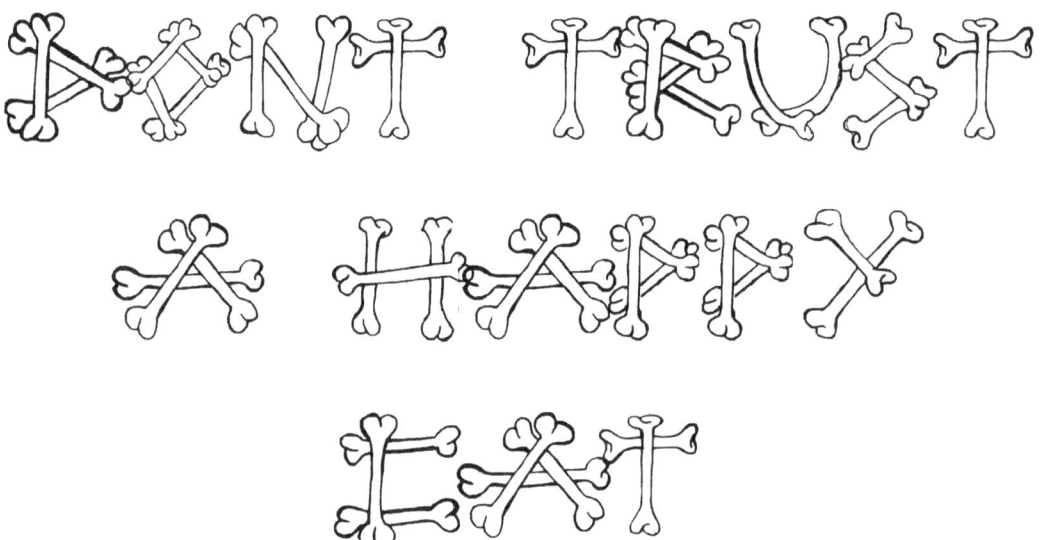

DONT TRUST A HAPPY CAT

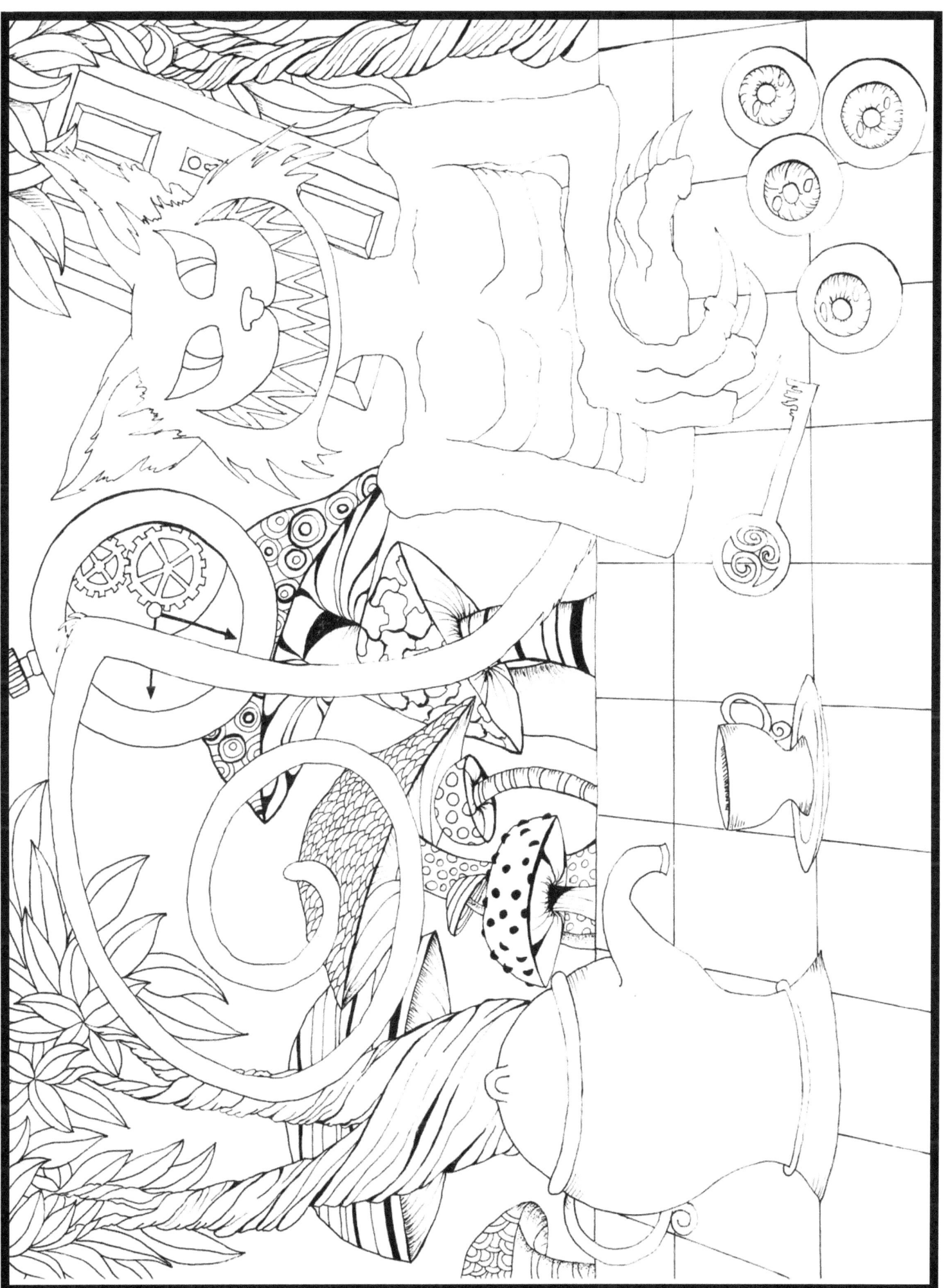

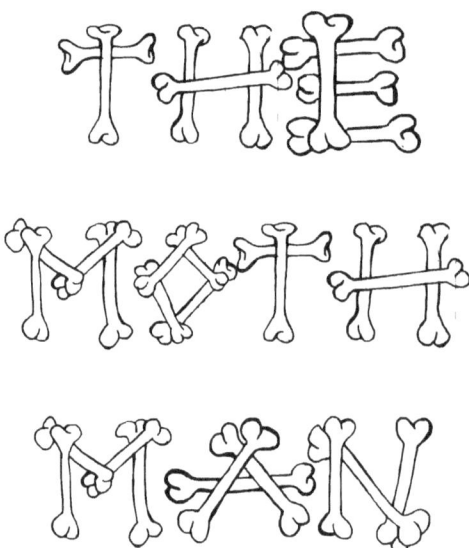

THE MOTH MAN

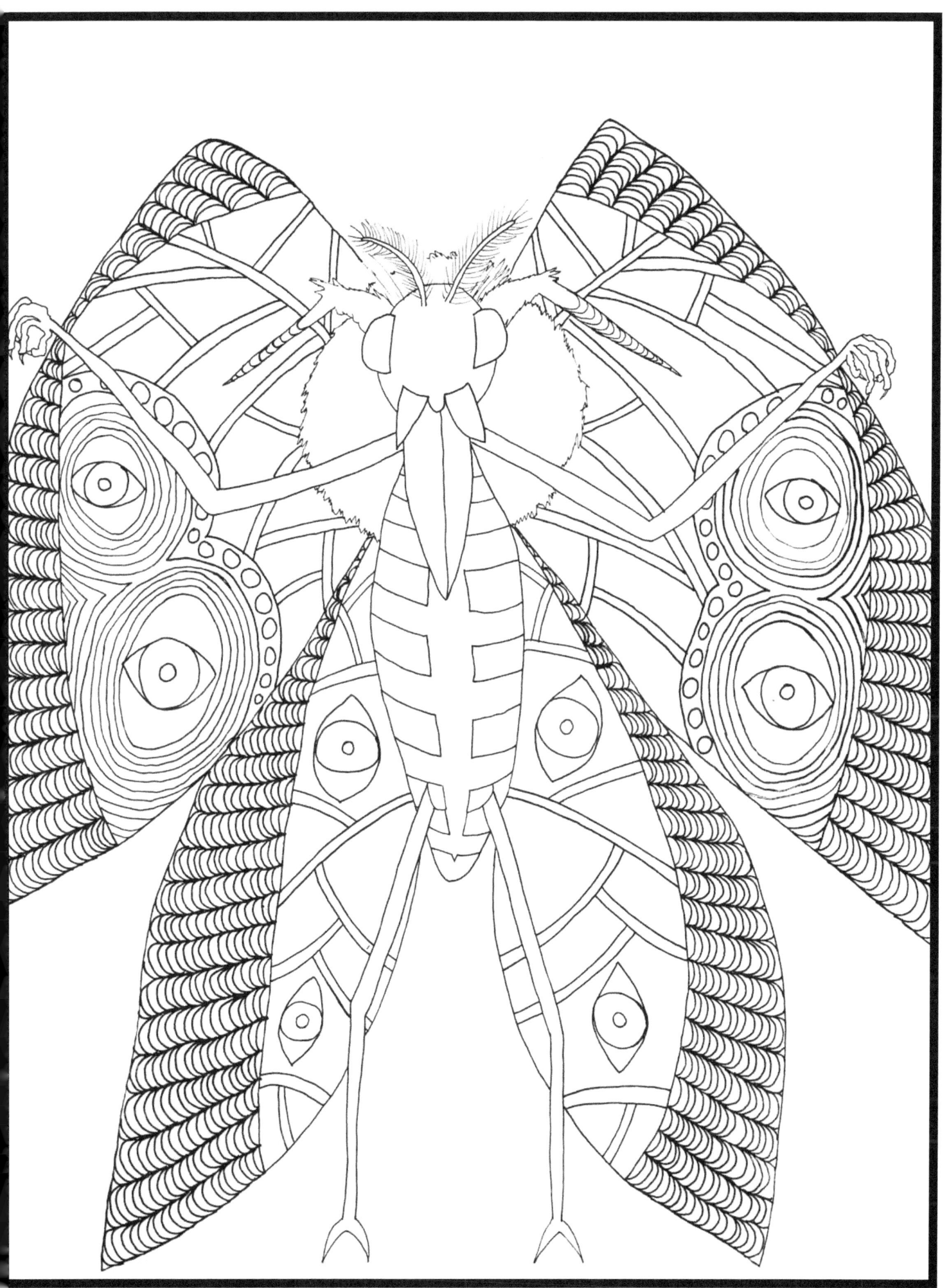

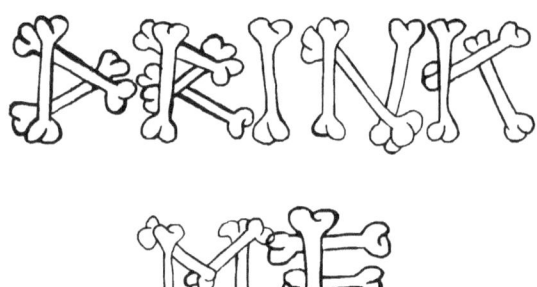

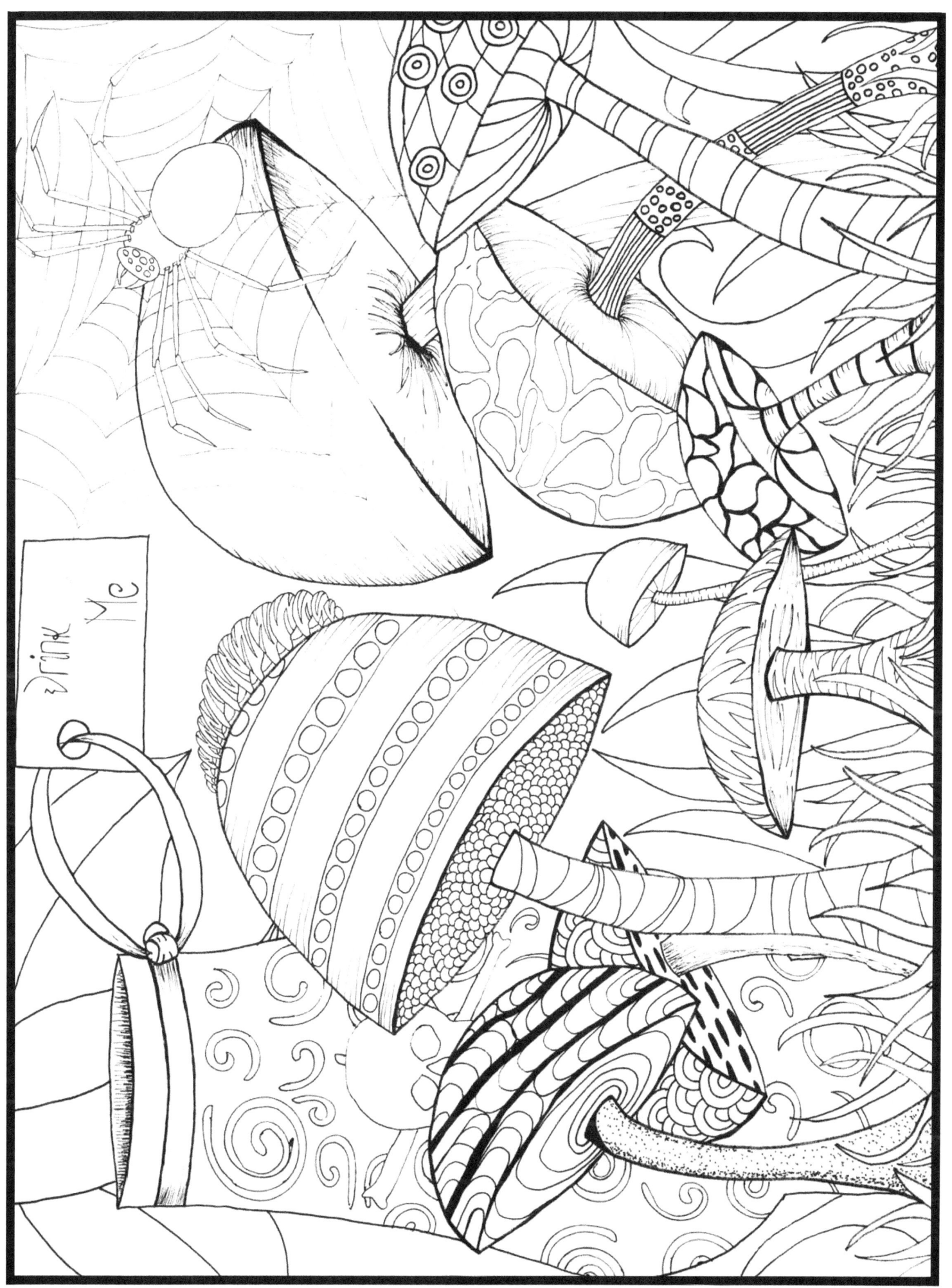

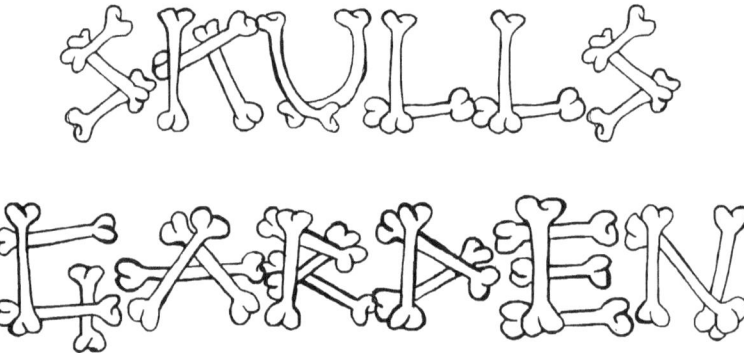

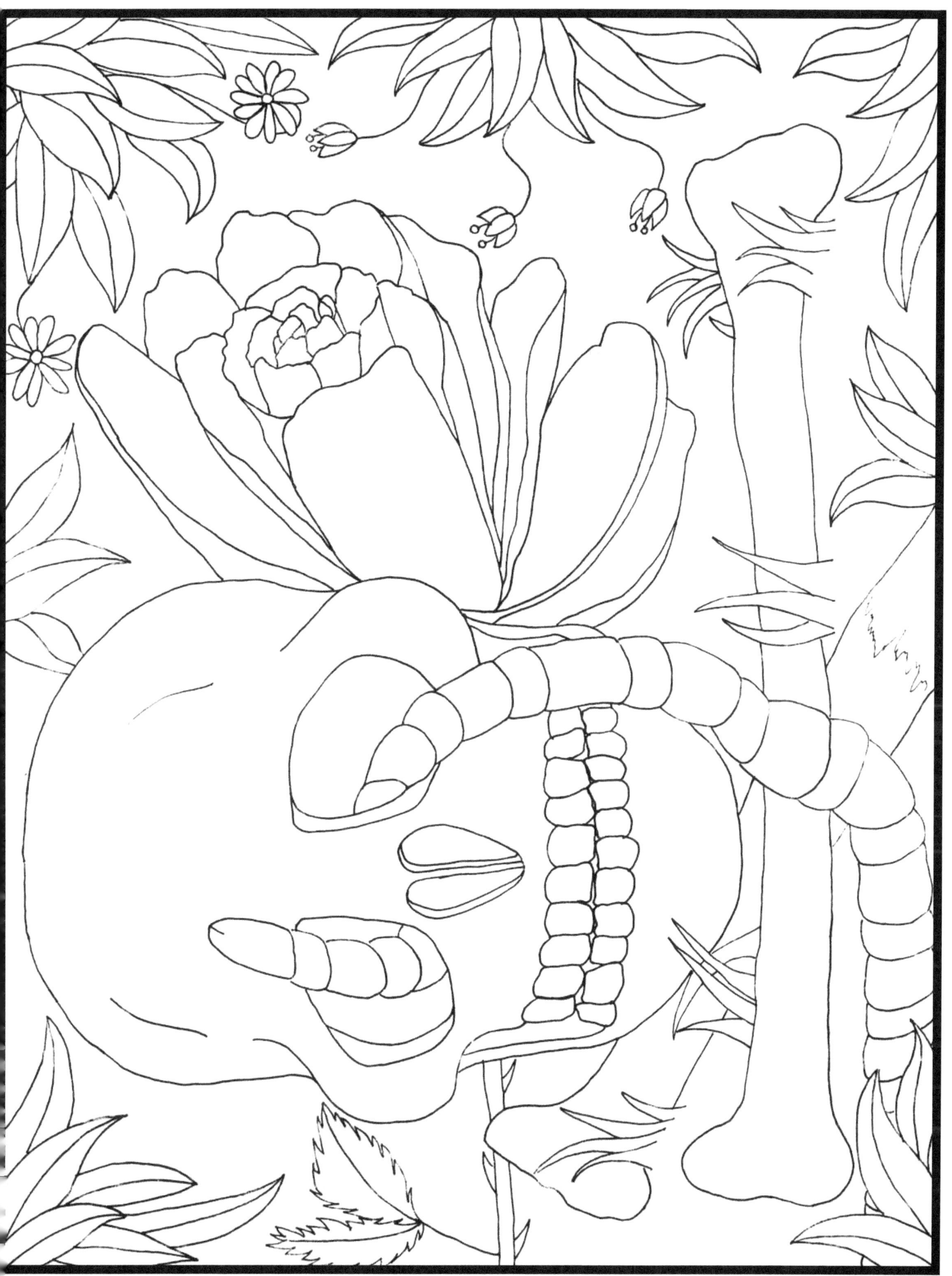

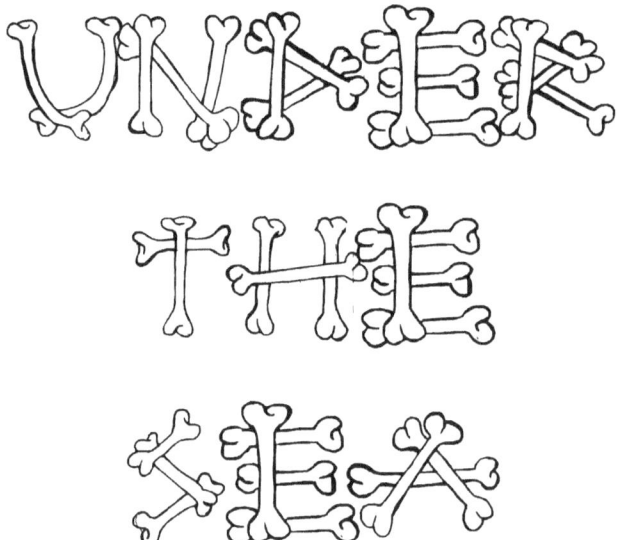

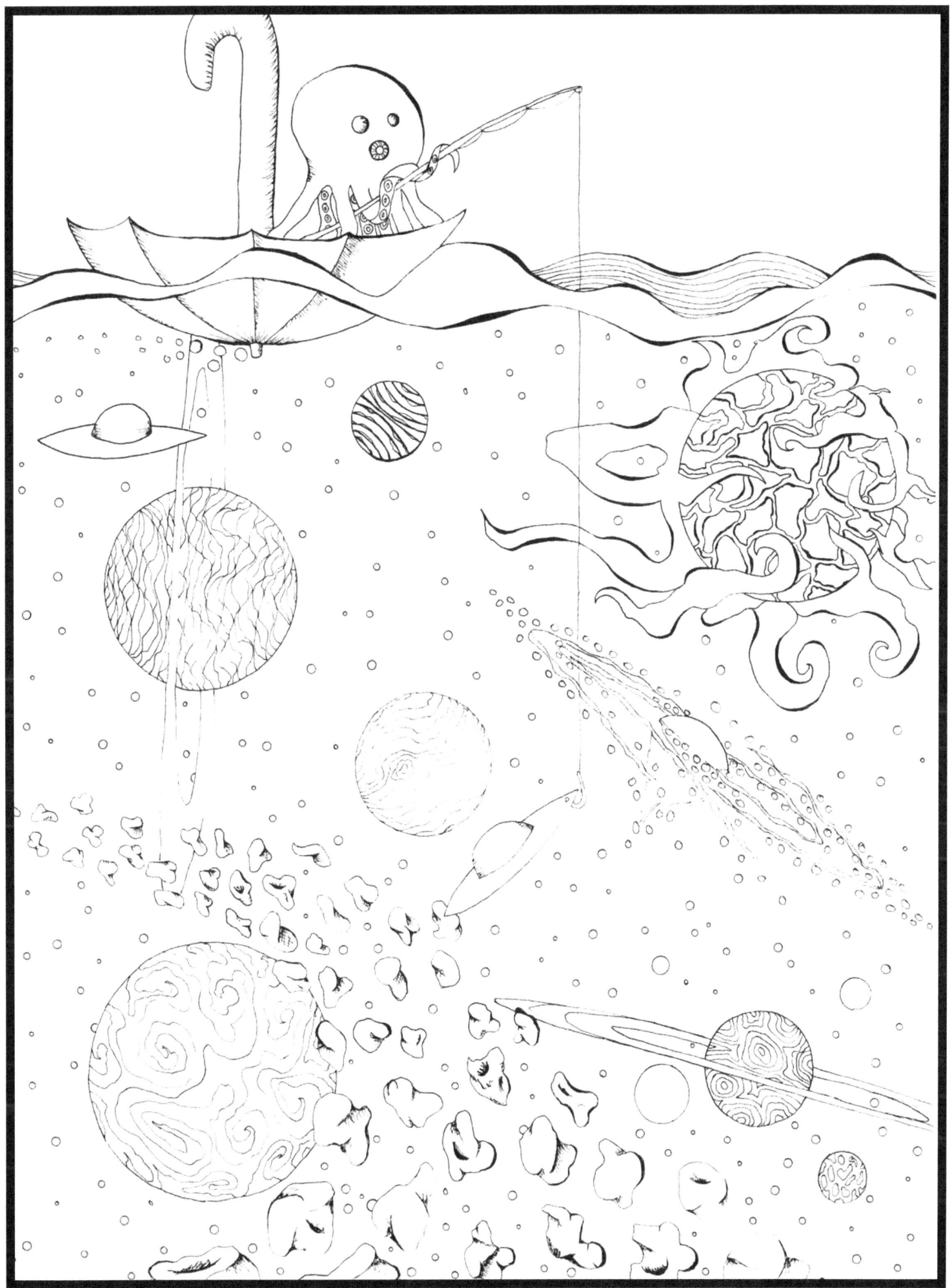

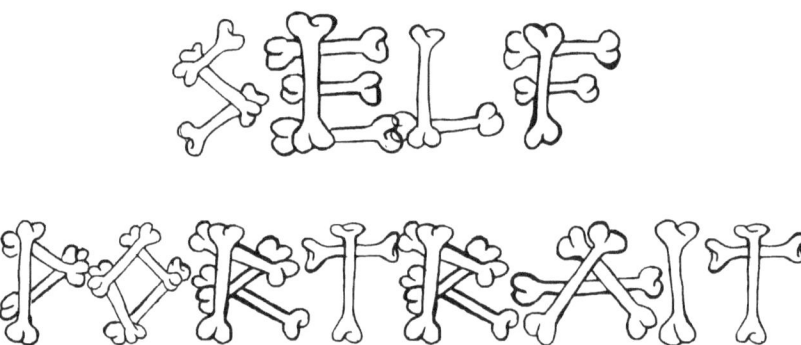

SELF PORTRAIT

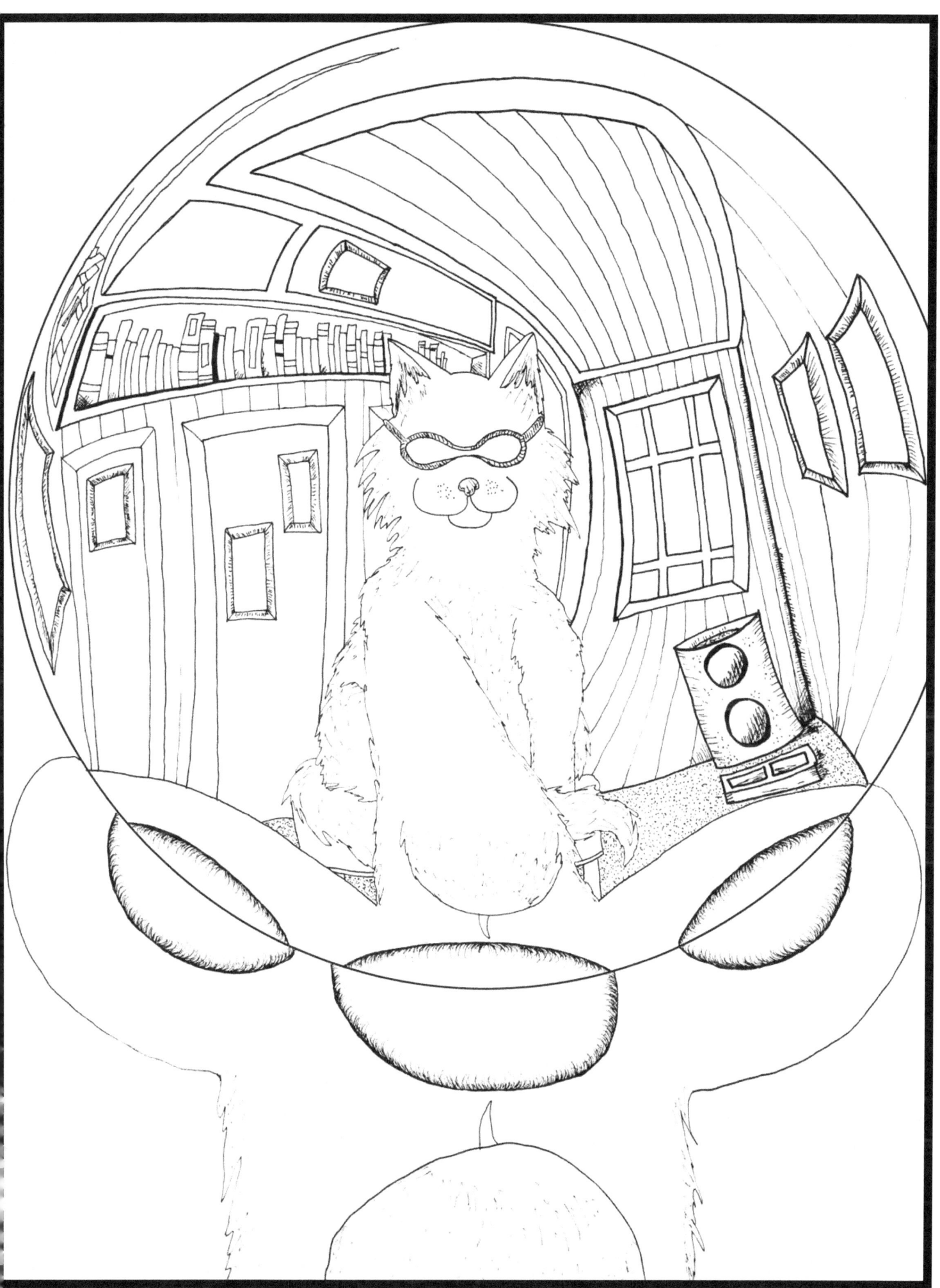

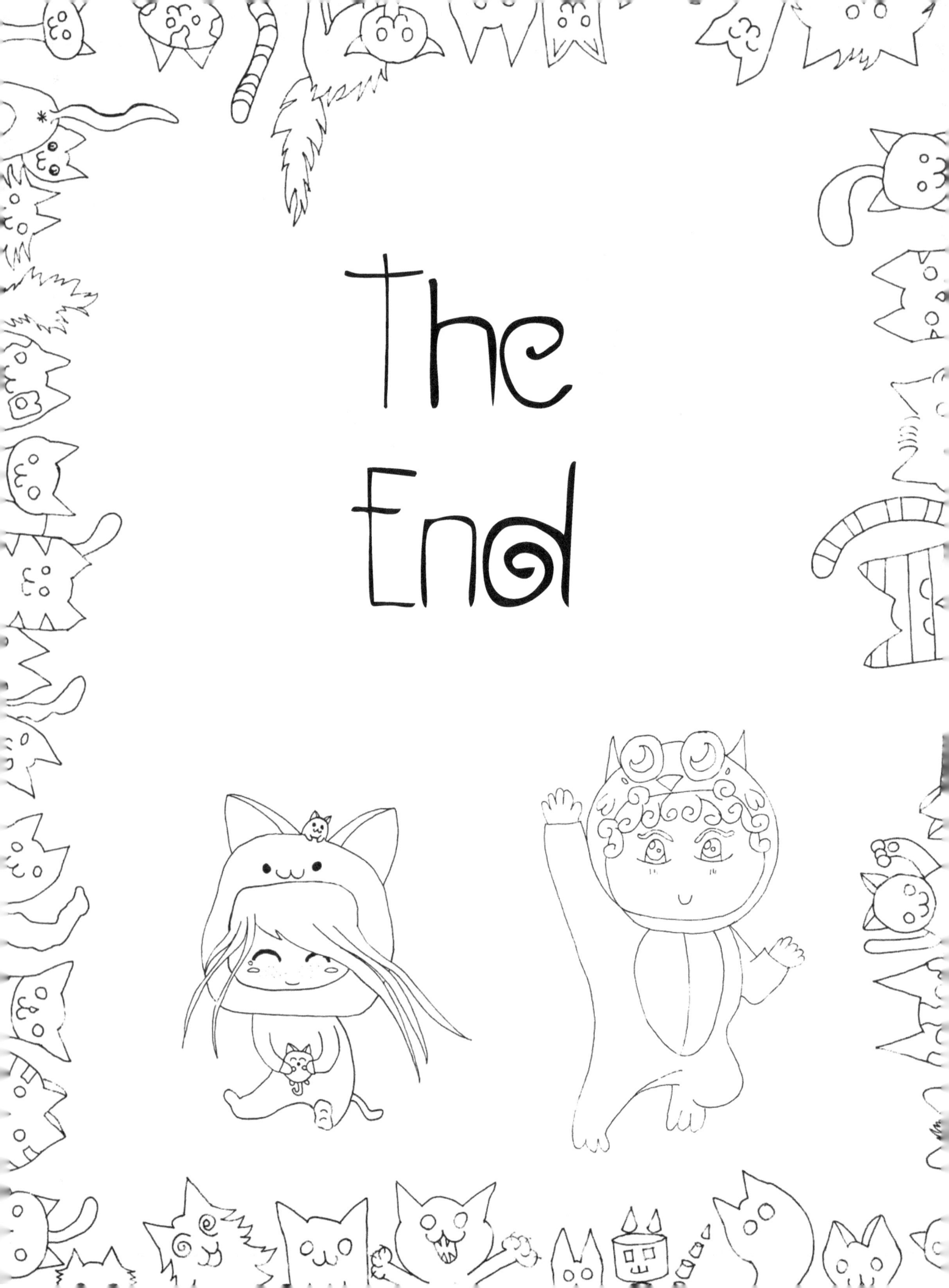

The
End

www.ingramcontent.com/pod-product-compliance
Lightning Source LLC
Chambersburg PA
CBHW081744220526
45468CB00008B/2226